THE HALF-KNOWN WORLD

THE HALF-KNOWN WORLD

On Writing Fiction

ROBERT
BOSWELL

Graywolf Press
SAINT PAUL, MINNESOTA

Publication of this volume is made possible in part by a grant provided by
the Minnesota State Arts Board, through an appropriation by the Minnesota
State Legislature; a grant from the Wells Fargo Foundation Minnesota; and
a grant from the National Endowment for the Arts, which believes that a
great nation deserves great art. Significant support has also been provided
by the Bush Foundation; Target; the McKnight Foundation; and other generous contributions from foundations, corporations, and individuals. To
these organizations and individuals we offer our heartfelt thanks.

Published by Graywolf Press
2402 University Avenue, Suite 203
Saint Paul, Minnesota 55114
All rights reserved.

www.graywolfpress.org

Published in the United States of America

ISBN 978-1-55597-504-3

2 4 6 8 9 7 5 3 1
First Graywolf Printing, 2008

Library of Congress Control Number: 2007940213

Cover design: Kimberly Glyder Design

Cover photograph: "Stephen Ascending" by Jade Nelson Boswell

CONTENTS

PREFACE

Like sex, reading is both a simple delight and a complex one, a nearly effortless pleasure that nonetheless rewards study and labor. Writing falls within the same general category—an activity that provides immediate booty and yet stands up to years of investigation. This book is meant to advance such an investigation. While the essays are aimed at working writers, I think serious readers will also find them worthwhile.

All of the essays may be read independently, but I've included at the beginning of each a list of the key stories and novels to which the essay refers. Ideally, of course, one would read the stories and novels before reading the essays. The reader will almost certainly understand the essays' arguments anyway; however, I have made no effort to conceal the plots. I've found that I cannot fully discuss a story while being coy about important plot elements. The essays may seem like "spoilers" if you've never read the fiction they analyze. My own experience suggests that the pleasures of plot are typically the least important of the reading experience. The best fiction is worthy of many return visits, even after you have the plot memorized. (The lists include only fiction; other sources are included in a complete list of works referenced at the back of the book. I do not list passing references to stories or novels unless the reference is crucial or reveals plot.)

Most of these essays evolved from lectures I've given at the Warren Wilson MFA Program for Writers. Many of them, in turn, started with classes I gave at New Mexico State University, Northwestern University, the Bread Loaf Writers' Conference, the University of Arizona, and the University of Houston. Portions of these essays have been published in *Puerto del Sol*, *Colorado Review*, *Bringing the Devil to His Knees*, and *The Story Behind the Story*, and I have delivered excerpts at the annual conferences of AWP (Association of Writers and Writing Programs). I am grateful to my colleagues, editors, and students at all of the above, and especially to Kevin McIlvoy, Steven Schwartz, Ellen Bryant Voigt, David Schweidel, Lindsay Armstrong, Katie Dublinski, Steve Orlen, Connie Voisine, Rus Bradburd, Susan Nelson, Alex Parsons, Charles Baxter, Peter Turchi, Tony Hoagland, and Antonya Nelson.

The Nephew by James Purdy
Who's Afraid of Virginia Woolf? by Edward Albee
Jesus' Son by Denis Johnson

THE HALF-KNOWN WORLD

-1-

I grew up on a tobacco farm on a county road that ran along a wooded ridge in western Kentucky. In winter, when the trees dropped their interference, we could catch glimpses of the Mississippi River from our car windows. Our town lay a few miles south of the farm, just below the confluence of the Mississippi and Ohio rivers. It would have been the first town Huck and Jim passed after missing their turn that foggy night. In our neck of the river, the breadth of the Mississippi exceeded a mile. It was a wide, moody, muddy deity. "Everything makes its way to the river," my father often said—once, I recall, on the occasion of our peeing together on the slope behind our shed.

My best friend lived on the same blacktop road. His name was Brady. He and I played together in the woods: cowboys and Indians, pirates and captains, the War Between the States—anything with a narrative. We had decided we would be writers when we grew up and we played in chapters, narrating in the third person, pausing to invent a new chapter heading whenever we reached a suitably mysterious moment. In the woods behind Brady's house, we stomped out a network of paths and constructed a tree house that overlooked a creek. Brady suggested we ought to one day follow the creek all the way to the river. We agreed that it would make a beautiful story, but the woods were dense with brush and briars. We never hiked very far beyond the beaten paths.

Snow came every winter, but the winter Brady and I were in third grade it arrived early and was followed by a hard freeze. The creek became solid, its gray surface resembling marble more than glass. Brady opened a chapter with "At last they had a clear path to the river," and we were off. Our narrative made us brave and neither of us was terribly bright. We set out on the ice for the great wide waters of the Mississippi.

We didn't tell anyone our plan. It wasn't part of the story.

Hiking on the frozen creek was unlike any of our other adventures. It was thrilling to be walking on water. It was also slippery, cold, and slow going. The ice made noises, as did the trees, and things beyond the trees we could not name. I did not at that time own sneakers. My school shoes had slick cardboard soles. I could slide long distances on the ice, but my feet were cold and I fell at regular intervals, as if to punctuate the stream's winding passage.

The creek meandered so much that the hike of a few miles became an odyssey. Walking kept off the chill, except about our faces and ears, where we felt the sting. After a while it began to snow, a frail and hesitant fall. The gray sky turned to pearl as it approached dusk, hedging into darkness. As the air cooled, the forest sounds grew sharper. The wincing of overhanging limbs became ominous. If the adults who endured our disappearance that afternoon are to be believed, we hiked for four hours.

It seemed to us much longer.

Our story faltered now and again, but we did not let it slip away. I began to wonder what we would do when we reached the Mississippi. In my mind, the center of the river rose up higher than the frozen banks and was rounded on top like a great unsheathed vein. I imagined standing before that vast expanse of ice and water, snow and sky. My legs—or perhaps my character's legs—wobbled at the thought. We were engaged with something enormous, I understood. I didn't have the right words to express what it was, but I felt it.

The dark gathered density while we walked along, cheerful and exalted and on the brink of terror. I do not recall much of our story line, but I do remember that Brady identified a flaw in our body of work. We never had any girls in our stories.

"It just isn't realistic," he noted.

I reluctantly concurred.

By this time we had no chance of getting home before the dark became as solid as the ice. We had not brought a flashlight or matches. Our parents would have realized by now that we had disappeared. Still, we kept walking and telling our tale. There was very little pretend left in it. We announced our progress to ourselves. We speculated on the comely woods. Our breath shimmered in the evening air, the little clouds that stories make.

We knew we were going to be in a lot of trouble with our parents. We thought too much of ourselves to believe we might get *spanked,* and we thought too much of our parents to believe we would be *beaten.* We would get *whupped.* We could not even deny that we had it coming. It might have been a comfort to consider the whupping we would get. It kept us from thinking we might die.

My father knew that forest in a way I never would. He had grown up on the same county road during the Great Depression. As a teenager, he had hunted in the bottomland to provide for his family. "We ate a lot of squirrel," he liked to say. Invariably, he would add, "It's good eating." His schooling was interrupted by war. He served in Italy and North Africa. When he returned, he married my mother and finished his degree. They tried living in Missouri and California, but my father kept returning to Kentucky. He would spend the latter part of his life in Arizona—a move dictated by the health of a child—but he would only ever know one place.

Luckily for Brady and me, we chose the right place to lose ourselves.

His deep voice seemed to descend from the heavens. "That's far enough, boys." I think it was my father who said it. He and

Brady's father stood on the creek bank beside poplar trees, each with his arms folded into the tucks of his jacket.

A wild topple of emotions brought a sudden pressure to my eyes. I felt relieved and deflated, rescued and arrested, fearful of punishment and angry at being caught, ashamed that I had made my father look for me and proud that we had covered such a distance. More than anything, though, I was amazed. We had told no one where we were going, and yet there were our fathers. Mine seemed to me something like omniscient. He had on his reversible hunting cap, the red plaid turned inside, showing only at the earflaps, a sift of snow on the bill.

Brady and I exchanged a look, but we said nothing as we tramped up the creek bank and through the trees. The men had come in separate cars, driving over a back road that had taken them within a dozen yards of the stream. Brady's father had a pickup. We owned a new Impala. It was not made for such roads, and I felt responsible for the muddy slush on its grille. Brady and I did not even wave good-bye, but trudged like convicts to our separate vehicles. Our winter story would remain unfinished.

Now and again, I find myself writing a story that revisits that illicit walk. None yet is precisely about those two boys and their fathers, but I often discover that the walk on the frozen creek has one way or another informed the plot, the setting, the characters, or even the structure of a story. I do not set out to re-create the walk, but the walk aroused in me the complicated and contradictory feelings that lend themselves to fiction.

I have grown to understand narrative as a form of contemplation, a complex and seemingly incongruous way of thinking. I come to know my stories by writing my way into them. I focus on the characters without trying to attach significance to their actions. I do not look for symbols. For as long as I can, I remain purposefully blind to the machinery of the story and only partially cognizant of the world the story creates. I work from a kind of half-knowledge.

In the drafts that follow, I listen to what has made it to the page. Invariably, things have arrived that I did not invite, and they are often the most interesting things in the story. By refusing to fully know the world, I hope to discover unusual formations in the landscape, and strange desires in the characters. By declining to analyze the story, I hope to keep it open to surprise. Each new draft revises the world but does not explain or define it. I work through many drafts, progressively abandoning the familiar. What I can see is always dwarfed by what I cannot know. What the characters come to understand never surpasses that which they cannot grasp. The world remains half-known.

In "The Art of Fiction," Henry James advises writers: "Try to be one of the people on whom nothing is lost." I work by the opposite means. I resist knowing until the story finally rubs my nose in it.

-2-

The illusion of people and place created by a story is the algebraic product of a writer's art and a reader's engagement. This world exists not on the page but in the reader's mind. The writer is responsible for the surface story of character and conflict, the evocation of a fictional reality (including the terms by which it operates), and the execution of a full narrative shape. If the writer's goal is literary fiction—a slippery term, but for the moment let's call it "fiction that aspires to be art"—then there are additional responsibilities. One of these, I'll argue, is the creation of a half-known world. To accomplish this, the writer must suggest a dimension to the fictional reality that escapes comprehension. The writer wishes to make his characters and their world known to the reader, and he simultaneously wishes to make them resonate with the unknown.

It may be easier to understand this argument if I start with stories that create fully known worlds.

The theme song to one of the most successful sitcoms in television history argues, "Sometimes you want to go where everybody knows your name, and they're always glad you came." This pretty much sums up the "situation" in most situation comedies. A sitcom offers an unchanging community to which the viewer is always welcome.

Cheers is a classic example of the static world of situation comedy. From week to week, the cast of characters remains essentially the same. The primary landscape does not change. In each episode every character merely repeats his defining characteristics. The range of what can happen is limited, guaranteed to be essentially comedic, and nothing that occurs in any individual episode will upset the reliable sameness. (This, of course, is the *opposite* goal of a literary short story, which promises some kind of change.) For the sitcom viewer, there is comfort in consistency and repetition. This community will remain unaltered, no matter what particular hell the viewer may be going through.

Now and then real life interferes with the sitcom—an actor dies or wants out of her contract—and the show is forced to accommodate, but Coach, the lovable bartender who was hit once too often by a fastball, is replaced by Woody, the Indiana farm hick who is as sweetly dumb as a plank. Even when something changes, it remains the same.

We can't predict exactly the rejoinder that Sam will make to Diane (or Diane's replacement), but we know the type of comment it will be, the relative degree of wit involved, and just how far it will go. Having our expectations almost perfectly met makes us feel knowing, possessively fond, and calm. These are our rewards for watching. After just a few episodes, the sitcom world is fully known. A character may have a secret, but it will be revealed before the half hour expires, and it will not change the way you think of him. The TV sitcom is an explicit medium: nothing that is under the surface can remain there for long.

While the sitcom is perhaps the clearest example of a fully known world, television dramas and most Hollywood movies are nearly its equal. Popular films work to give you the sense that you are being shown *everything*. As a result, character motivations tend to come from the big categories, such as "They killed my family, so I will get them," or "He saved my life, so I like him." Every action is motivated by something that you witness firsthand or that is explained to you.

To make something fully known is to make it unreal. Think of Disneyland, think of the speeches of politicians, think of McDonald's, Burger King, Kentucky Fried Chicken. The fast-food goal is not to give you a great meal but to give you exactly what you expect. There is comfort in this, especially for children, for people traveling abroad, and for people whose lives are in upheaval. People in a crisis long for KFC and *Seinfeld*, McDonald's and Arnold Schwarzenegger, Pizza Hut and a president who says, "We are good. They are evil."

It should be no surprise that the fully known worlds presented on television and in commercial movies are populated by stereotypes. To call a character a type is to say that he's so true to a group of characters that he is indistinguishable from all the others in that group. Here's another definition of stereotype: any character that is fully known.

-3-

Imagine a play set in the wilderness, a serious play by an important playwright. The stage set is elaborate. It includes a mammoth tree and a stream with real water that runs across the front of the stage and feeds a small pond. A few minutes into the play, thunder sounds and it actually begins to rain, water cascading down from above and landing in the stream. It is an impressive spectacle; however, sitting there in the audience, I feel myself slip out of the drama to wonder about the complicated sprinkling and drainage system. In the second act, one character tortures another by dragging him to the pond and holding his head under the water. At this point, I bounce entirely out of the play. I catch myself wondering whether he has a straw under there by which to breathe.

The rain and pond interfere with the audience's ability to enter the play's world. They are too literal for the medium. You will not be surprised to hear that the playwright had recently been writing

Hollywood screenplays. Returning to the stage, he confused the nature of film with the nature of drama. Serious theater, like serious fiction, is a medium of implication. A play succeeds by making you see what is not there. Two actors staring as if through a window create not only the glass but also the landscape. In the same fashion, characters acting on grudges held for decades suggest a past and create a history, one that may never be made explicit but that resonates in their actions. The audience must participate in the creation of the world. The job of a literary play is to use the visible to suggest the invisible. When the two are properly balanced, the audience becomes fully absorbed in the creative work.

Now imagine the wilderness play is made into a film, and the director decides to *pretend* to dunk the actor in a make-believe pond. The audience would hoot. The Hollywood movie is an explicit medium and it demands that we see the head held beneath the water, preferably with a submerged view of desperate bubbles escaping flared nostrils.

Fiction writers often make the same mistake as the playwright in his wilderness play. They confuse the half-known world of literary fiction with the fully known worlds of popular film or TV sitcom. Even textbooks designed to teach fiction writing suffer from this confusion. Novice writers are advised to make a list of traits that define a character or a specific setting *prior* to embarking on a story. Here's how one handbook puts it: "The writer sets the game in motion by knowing the fictional personages so well that every move they make, every word they speak, every thought they have grows from a kind of intimate biography." This is standard advice and it is often accompanied by a list of questions to answer, such as the following:

1. What is the birthday of your main character? Where was your character born? What is your character's economic background? And so on.

2. How tall is your character? How much does your character weigh? What color hair? Etc.

3. What is your character's job? How long has your character had this job? How well is your character paid?

4. What does your character do with his or her free time? Does your character have a hobby?

5. What makes your character angry? What makes your character sad?

6. What does your character want from life?

Similar lists are encouraged for setting, asking you to name everything in the character's apartment, every book on the character's shelves, and so on. Evidently, each character and setting should get this treatment.

I take issue with the idea that the writer must know the characters "so well that every move they make, every word they speak, every thought they have grows from a kind of intimate biography." I'll extend the argument to cover similar counsel on creating settings. I don't believe that it's a good idea to make a list of everything that might appear in a room before you set a scene in it.

What the lists imply is that you must know the characters and their world quite thoroughly to write about them. Okay, that *sounds* reasonable, but it's not true. Moreover, it's often a bad idea or, at best, an unfortunate simplification. The listing of characteristics in advance of real narrative exploration tends to cut a character off at the knees. Such a character may be complicated but is rarely complex. Moreover, such characters tend to become narrower as the narrative progresses. The writer who has typed in the answers to the preceding questions may feel knowing, possessively fond, and calmly confident; but he may find it difficult to let the character break out of these imaginative restraints.

-4-

Even Hollywood doesn't want to be accused of using stereotypes. Typically in movies, there is an effort to contradict some aspect of the type. They will force the stereotype to do something that doesn't fit. This method has resulted in the creation of bizarre metatypes that you will instantly recognize, such as the granny who looks aged and retiring, and yet speaks in four-letter words and rides a Harley; or the macho supercop who pauses in his apartment while changing his bloody shirt to study the chessboard and the game he is playing long-distance with a professor genius. Fiction writers who attempt to deal with a stereotype by merely disrupting the character's adherence to type are like the playwright who puts a pond onstage: they are confusing their medium.

The better method is to suggest the parts of the character that are, by most standards, invisible. In other words, assume that the attributes that make the character a type are merely the surface features. Another way to put it: write the character so that his actions and dialogue suggest that the reader can only ever half-know him.

For example, you discover that you have the following stereotype: a dumb jock. His name is Ron. You can't avoid stereotype by having Ron teach a seminar in feminist theory or by showing him reading Wittgenstein. Instead, your task is to inhabit his dumbness and his obedience to the physical, and find within them the residual mystery of being. Instead of including the unlikely and unexpected, include the details one might expect but cannot anticipate. Ron's desires may be predictable, but his way of thinking about them, approaching them, categorizing them, dwelling on them, resisting them, and acting on them should permit you to make the reader forget that, on the surface, this character has the appearance of a type. At some point, the reader will only think of Ron as Ron. In fact, Ron Patimkin in Philip Roth's *Goodbye, Columbus* is just such a character. Nothing in his behavior contradicts the type, and yet Roth makes him vivid, specific, and unforgettable.

Sometimes in a novel (or in a play) characters appear first as types. As the novel progresses, the writer works to make the character an individual. This work entails, I am arguing, the *unknowing* of the character. You can measure how successfully you've re-vealed a character by the extent to which his acts, words, history, and thoughts *fail* to explain him, creating instead a character that is, at once, identifiable and unknowable.

-5-

Late in James Purdy's strange, beautiful novel *The Nephew,* Alma Mason decides she must tell her brother that the boy they raised has been killed in Korea and there are no remains to ship home. Alma says: "There should have been something left. . . . There should have been something *from* him for us. And I never knew him, Boyd. I only loved him. I never *knew* Cliff."

This is the culminating episode in the novel for Alma Mason. From the beginning, she has been characterized as a bossy, criti-cal, and ungrateful person, a self-important and self-justifying know-it-all. If she remained the character she is at the opening of the book, she would likely seem like a stereotype by novel's end. But over the course of the narrative, she discovers by increments how little she really knows, until she arrives at this moment of humility: *I never knew him. I only loved him.*

The novel portrays Alma's painful unlearning of her nephew and her neighbors. She has lived under the assumption that she knows her world quite thoroughly, but she has only ever partially comprehended any of it. The reader discovers that Alma has made erroneous assumptions about every neighbor on the block. By the end, she arrives at a new and mysterious place, even though it is the same neighborhood where she has spent most of her life; but now it is only half-known. This does not make her world smaller but larger, as the surface reality now represents only a portion of existence, and everywhere there are signifiers of the other half.

One of the things that I love about this novel is how pow-erfully *absence* functions. Cliff, the nephew, is absent from the beginning, but the quality of his absence changes as the novel pro-gresses. At first, he is gone and writing dilatory letters that have an adequate number of lines and nice penmanship but say very little. Then he goes "missing in action" and the correspondence ends. The official letter announcing his disappearance is short and has misspellings, and it says more than his aunt and uncle can comprehend. Alma accuses her brother of believing that Cliff is dead. Boyd angrily denies it. Note that they are not arguing about whether the boy is alive or dead but the extent to which each *believes* he is dead. Initially, Cliff is "more dead" to Boyd than to Alma, but this balance will teeter and shift, and even after there is no doubt about his death, the quality of his absence continues to change as new things about him are revealed.

Alma decides to create a memorial for her nephew—a journal and scrapbook—in which she will rediscover the lost child. She is undecided about what to include and investigates her nephew's life in order to represent it accurately. Everything she discovers contradicts what she thought she knew. Ultimately, the memorial is composed of blank pages.

The novel ends as follows:

"Did you hear what I said?" Boyd asked. "Sometimes I think your hearing is nearly as bad as mine." He could only see her nod, not hear her voice.

By their practice of sitting in the dark, only their white hair, which at times shone almost like phosphorescence, betokened each other's presence.

Through open windows there came the faint delicious perfume of azaleas. The courthouse clock struck ten.

The final line of dialogue in the book—Alma's response to her brother—goes unheard by Boyd in his half-deafness, and the reader too fails to hear it, left instead in the dimming room as the night erases it, luminous hair floating in the dark amid the perfume of azaleas and the sounding of the clock. Alma and Boyd are half-visible, their exchange is half-heard, the evening's fall arriving in a world half-known. In this utterly ordinary domestic moment, Purdy creates resonant mystery.

-6-

A fully known world is devoid of mystery. There are often plenty of secrets, but ultimately all you can do with a secret is to reveal it. The arguments against using secrets in literary work are familiar to most writers. The character possessing a dark secret that will remain concealed until the novel's end is a familiar character, prone to sentimentality and caricature. Moreover, after a long buildup, it's difficult to reveal something that will genuinely affect a reader. Such revelation most often turns out to be deflating, limiting, manipulative, melodramatic, or merely explanatory. Yet there is no denying that many literary works use secrets successfully. In Edward Albee's play *Who's Afraid of Virginia Woolf?* the audience is astonished to discover in the final minutes of the performance that George and Martha's "blonde-eyed, blue-haired" son is a creation of their shared imagination.

A synopsis of the play might make George and Martha seem dangerously close to stereotypes: the bitter, failed, drunken academic and his disappointed, acerbic, alcoholic wife—the ineffectual intellectual and the woman who's making him pay for it. Albee has no interest in contradicting these types; instead, his play dwells on the details of George's bogged-down career, it swims in their consumption of alcohol, and it revels in their gloriously nasty marital accusations. While their surface traits never contradict type, no one on the planet thinks of George and Martha as stereotypes.

After the doorbell chimes but before answering the door, George says to Martha, "Just don't start in on the bit about the kid, that's all." He's talking about their son. "Just leave the kid out of this," he says, which, of course, encourages her to do the opposite. Every reference to their son is either vague or enigmatic;

occasionally there's one that's downright baffling, as when George explains to Nick, "All I said was, our son . . . the apple of our three eyes, Martha being a Cyclops . . . our son is a bean bag, and you get testy."

That George and Martha have a secret is clear, and the audience becomes certain that it concerns their son. But the nature of the secret is hard to pin down. Moreover, the play aggressively investigates the relationship between truth and illusion, which keeps the viewer off-balance and recalibrating. Statements initially thought to be factual are later called into question, and the figurative dimension of the couple's language suggests realms of the unknown.

> GEORGE: Martha, I gave you the prize years ago. . . . There
>   isn't an abomination award going that you. . . .
> MARTHA: I swear . . . if you existed I'd divorce you. . . .

George and Martha constantly question whether the other is real, whether the other is human. Because the actors playing the roles are indisputably real and the play is conspicuously realistic, the insistent contradiction in their dialogue not only characterizes this gargantuan pair but creates a mythic sense of George and Martha and the viciously tender vision they share. It is not until the very end of the play that the audience realizes that one of the characters does not really exist, except in the imagination of this particular husband and wife.

When every assertion has a shadow, a shadow world eventually emerges. George and Martha's surface life is lively and layered in allusion, fed by bitterness and anger, and yet it conjures up another world they share, another kind of existence, also rich, also layered in allusion. While this other life is invisible, its evocation is far more present onstage than the artificial rain of the play I mentioned earlier. In fact, Albee finds ways to make the "other side" tangible.

Shortly after Nick and Honey arrive, Nick tries to compliment a painting on the living room wall, but George won't permit his unctuous civility.

> NICK: It's got a . . . a. . . .
> GEORGE: A quiet intensity?
> NICK: Well, no . . . a . . . .
> GEORGE: Oh. *(Pause)* Well, then, a certain noisy relaxed
>   quality, maybe?

When George decides to apologize, he says, "I *am* sorry. . . . What it is, actually, is it's a pictorial representation of the order of Martha's mind." Here George insists that a prop on the stage represents something from the other side. This moment is related to what Purdy does in his final paragraphs (although to very different effect): presenting a visual representation of the invisible.

George creates an accident that "kills" their son, and the death in one realm creates grief in the other. The play ends with George singing, "Who's afraid of Virginia Woolf . . . ," and Martha responding, "I . . . am . . . George. . . . I . . . am. . . ." The chant itself is a complex mantra, a child's recitation combined with a literary allusion, the big bad wolf made over into a great and difficult writer much studied in academia, a brilliant inventor of imaginary worlds whose life ended in suicide. When Martha responds to the chant in this final exchange, she is talking directly from the other side. Having created for themselves a multifaceted invisible life, Martha and George intuit that the loss of their fantastic son calls into question their ability to get by in the "real" world.

When the secret of their son is revealed, it suggests that the invisible world of George and Martha is even more substantial than we had guessed. They become *more* mysterious. This is the key thing to understand: in literary works, secrets function to the extent that their revelation creates an equal portion of mystery. The world then remains half-known. The revelation that their son is a fabrication is stunning, and it answers some of the audience's questions; but it does not explain the mystery of George and Martha.

-7-

In *The Nephew,* there is a secret concerning $4,000 that goes through a number of permutations. It creates more mystery each time a new fact is revealed. At first, the mystery is where the money came from, and then it's why the cash was given to the absent nephew, Cliff. At one point, the reader thinks he understands something that Boyd and Alma are afraid to face—that Cliff posed for money, that he may have had a homosexual relationship with a neighbor, or even a paid sexual relationship. But the reader is not going to be entirely right, either. Another neighbor accounts for the money in a manner that makes her character larger and less defined, and the first neighbor will clarify matters in a fashion that, in turn, changes the way we understand Cliff's relationship to the town and to his aunt and uncle. Each time we unmask a secret, new mysteries emerge.

Purdy leaves a good deal of the story up for interpretation. There is a subtext about people acting on hidden desires, a fire whose source is never fully explained, and a fatal automotive accident that may be the product of a character's unconscious wish. The world of the novel seems quite distinct and knowable initially, but Purdy works to progressively enlarge the unknown.

Denis Johnson's *Jesus' Son* uses an opposite strategy. This story cycle tracks the movement of the main character (known to us as Fuckhead) from his life as a drug addict and fuckup to a much different life, free of drugs. This is the surface story, and it inscribes a familiar narrative arc; however, this is in no way a familiar narrative. In its recognizable form, as we see it so often in TV and film, the movement from addiction to being drug-free is an uplifting story that permits the viewer to leave the theater with uncomplicated feelings. But in the half-known world of this book, the narrative is less clear-cut, and the reader understands that the character's movement involves difficult trade-offs.

The opening to *Jesus' Son* establishes that Fuckhead (he has no "real" name) exists in an unknowable state of being: ". . . I rose up sopping wet from sleeping under the pouring rain, and something less than conscious." We discover that he is alone in a storm and hitchhiking, and the first moments of the narrative are both before and after the accident. Even as the narrative clarifies the situation, it enlarges the unknown:

> The downpour raked the asphalt and gurgled in the ruts. My thoughts zoomed pitifully. The travelling salesman had fed me pills that made the linings of my veins feel scraped out. My jaw ached. I knew every raindrop by its name. I sensed everything before it happened. I knew a certain Oldsmobile would stop for me even before it slowed, and by the sweet voices of the family inside it I knew we'd have an accident in the storm.

From the first page forward, Fuckhead is having lyrical premonitions and recollections. Johnson's strategy is to insist on immediate immersion in a half-known world, which he accomplishes by means of a narrator high on drugs and a narrative voice that is simultaneously lyrical and portentous, as well as comic and self-mocking. The movement over the course of the book to a life without drugs leaves Fuckhead better off physically but longing for access to the unknown, to mystery.

Since this strategy demands evidence of the unknown from the very beginning, Johnson's descriptions simultaneously suggest the known and undercut it: "Under Midwestern clouds like great grey brains we left the superhighway with a drifting sensation. . . ." After the car crash, Fuckhead finds himself holding a baby in the rain when a motorist stops:

"Is everybody dead?" he asked.

"I can't tell who is and who isn't," I admitted.

A few moments later, the motorist asks if the baby is a boy. Fuck-head doesn't know. Our narrator cannot tell who is alive and who is dead, and cannot distinguish gender; meanwhile, the world of his pulsing brain inhabits the skies. Dream and reality don't ex-actly trade places but share space.

The physical world is often grim in *Jesus' Son*, but the narra-tor's vision is equally often lyric, even ecstatic. The following is from the second story in the book, "Two Men," and it describes a place Fuckhead visits at the request of a stranger who may or may not be able to speak or hear:

> It was a small wooden house with two posts for a clothes-line out front. The grass had grown up and been crushed by the snows and then uncovered by the thaw. Without bothering to knock I went around to the window and looked in. There was one chair all by itself at an oval table. The house looked abandoned, no curtains, no rugs. All over the floor there were shiny things I thought might be spent flashbulbs or empty bullet casings. But it was dark and nothing was clear. I peered around until my eyes were tired and I thought I could make out designs all over the floor like the chalk outlines of victims or markings for strange rituals.

I cannot imagine anyone coming to write this description if he first made an exhaustive list of everything one might find in the room.

Here's a description of a character excerpted and pasted to-gether from the same story:

> Several ghost-complected women were lying around. One just like those came through the door from that room and

stood looking at the three of us with her mascara blurred and her lipstick kissed away. She wore a skirt but not a blouse, just a white bra like someone in an undies ad in a teenage magazine. But she was older than that. Looking at her I thought of going out in the fields with my wife back when we were so in love we didn't know what it was. She wiped her nose, a sleepy gesture. . . . The woman hurt me. She looked so soft and perfect, like a mannequin made of flesh, flesh all the way through.

No writer could get such a description from a biography created by answering the typical list of questions offered in handbooks.

In the fully known world of movies and TV, we know that drugs are bad for you. In the half-known world of *Jesus' Son,* drugs are still bad for you but that does not mean they have no value. For Fuckhead, drug use is about tapping into a world that contains a rapturous and illusive sense of spiritual mystery—and this other world is what gives substance to *Jesus' Son.* Near the end of the book Fuckhead works to get straight, but it's clear that he's losing admission to something extraordinary.

In the final story, Fuckhead is a member of Narcotics Anonymous and a group for recovering heroin addicts and AA. He has a steady job at a home for disabled people. About his inner life, he says: "I was a whimpering dog inside, nothing more than that." One day while walking to the bus stop he hears a woman singing in her shower. It sets something off in him:

I thought of mermaids: the blurry music of falling water, the soft song from the wet chamber. The dusk was down, and the heat came off the hovering buildings. It was rush hour, but the desert sky has a way of absorbing the sounds of traffic and making them seem idle and small. Her voice was the clearest thing coming to my ears.

She sang with the unconsciousness, the obliviousness, of a castaway.

He winds up peeking in the woman's window. She's naked, but it isn't her body that keeps him looking until the sweep of her husband's headlights sends him home. He becomes obsessed with watching her and her husband, and, while it may be true that Fuckhead is trying to understand how it is that people go about having a life, it is also true that he has found access to another world, another kind of mystery—and it is for this that he longs.

-8-

When the reader's experience of a story results in a world that is too fully known, the story fails. I want to offer five categories of failure.

Category One: The Leaning Story. The world of a story may be too fully known because it leans too heavily on an existing system of beliefs. Imagine, for example, that Flannery O'Connor had written about Christian grace in a literal and ham-handed fashion. "A Good Man Is Hard to Find" might end with the manifestation of Christ peeping over the Misfit's shoulder at the grandmother. By speaking the appropriate beatitude, Christ encourages the grandmother's final comment to the Misfit. The reader would have to accept very specific religious beliefs, or the story wouldn't work.

Change that system of beliefs from the theological to the political. Imagine a story wherein it turns out that the root of all evil is a specific political party. However true this may seem to the writer, it won't make for good fiction. It doesn't permit the reader a place to stand and make her own judgments. Remove the political party and substitute the evils of television, the evils of a patriarchal culture, the evils of Daddy or Mommy—or any of the other specific entities against which a writer may rant.

The most common leaning story I see is one wherein the writer presents a vision of the world based on the tenets of contemporary psychology. In such stories, characters are symptomatic, and the reader's job is to diagnose them. They're not wild, but bipolar; they're not erratic and driven, they're OCD; they're not fucked-up, they're codependent. These diagnoses are offered as explanations, as if by knowing the correct psychological labels we have revealed the characters.

Category Two: The Cinematographer. Writers whose stories fall into this category have made the same kind of mistake as the author of the wilderness play. The stories borrow from the explicit media without recognizing that they work in an implied medium. Such stories cruise along the surface of the characters' world. Often they have an existential feel to them, but the characters are rarely concerned with the mysteries of existence, and such mysteries never seriously inform the stories. One type may pay great attention to possessions as a way to inform the reader that material possessions do not make for a rich life. But merely pointing a narrative camera at the Gucci shoes, the Ralph Lauren suit, and the gold Rolex watch does not adequately tell a story or convey a theme.

Stories in this category often rely heavily on the road trip for narrative development, but they read like travelogues posing as stories. If the stories have a metaphor, it will likely be heavy-handed. (One man in a car says to the driver, "You know this is a dead-end street." The driver replies, "I know." On down the road they ramble.) Writers like Ann Beattie or Mary Gaitskill or Denis Johnson often inspire these stories, but they are not really modeled after the work of these writers but after movies or TV shows that have similar situations. So Johnson's story "Emergency" from *Jesus' Son* may inspire the writer, but *ER* winds up being the model.

Category Three: The Bastard. A story may fail because the writer has made up his mind about the characters before any words reach the page. There is no room for the reader to resist the judgment because the events of the story prove the judgments wholly right. Often, the writer is working from personal experience, and his guilt is demanding that the character (his surrogate) be judged harshly. It seems that the writer understands he has messed up the best relationship of his life, and so he writes a story to prove what a stupid bastard he is. This is another kind of rant. The writer isn't exploring the experience; he's condemning himself.

Category Four: The Hipper-Than-Thou Story. Some stories suffer from being smug, and what is smugness but the assumption of a knowledge that is actually beyond one's reach? These stories are like the bastard stories, except the writer is proud of what his character is doing. It may be something noble or something awful; it doesn't matter. The story is self-congratulatory. (Note that the writer is responsible for the self-congratulation; many wonderful characters think the world of themselves while their stories suggest otherwise.) In a small variation, the story will include details that show the main character quite genuinely knows what's what concerning the current scene in fashion, drugs, or social manners. In such stories, this knowledge is deemed valuable.

Category Five: The Slogging Plod. This is the most common failed story and the most difficult to address. It is the story written by a writer who simply knows too much about the reality that the story wishes to portray; he understands his characters and their motivations too clearly, too logically, and too early; he has researched the material too categorically and completely; he comprehends where the story is going too correctly. He knows all of these things so well that the novel can only trudge forward, even though the language may be clear, the writing crisp, the authority impeccable. The narrative is typically dull: completely imagined, lavishly detailed, cleverly articulated, but sloggingly dull. The mountains of detail do not accumulate productively. Instead, they flatten the fiction with their weight. The characters tend to be motivated by explicit and logical reasons and nothing else; these novels ignore the unexplainable, the quirky, the unconscious—the human slippage that makes people large and contradictory and fascinating.

-9-

If I were to write a how-to primer for the creation of characters, I would put together a different set of questions than those typically posed. It might go something like this:

1. What did your character forget to do this morning?
2. Why does your character think he ought to be fired?
3. What recent mistake vaguely reminds your character of a previous mistake she can't name?
4. What stupid thing kept her awake last night?
5. If you met your character in a bar, what would she think of you? In what ways would she be right? What would she get wrong? What would she see about you that you don't yet understand about yourself?

These questions won't explain anything or anybody, but they may give you a handle by which you can pull yourself into this character's life. You do not know what the character wants, but you may have enough that you can begin exploring the character in a narrative, and you may eventually discover it.

The final question—what would your character think of you?—is meant to remind you of your complicity in the creative act. The discoveries you make about your characters work best if they involve searching that makes you uncomfortable, that forces you to face something you don't want to face, something that makes you want to flee—or at least shut off your laptop and go for a walk. Your job, of course, is to strap yourself in and keep writing. You've reached the point in the story where you have the opportunity to create something real. You're stepping onto terrain you only half-know. This is where you need to be. There can be no discovery in a world where everything is known. A crucial part of the writing endeavor is the practice of remaining in the dark.

-10-

My father and I sat in the dark of the idling car. He motioned for Brady's father to go first. We would take longer to get out of the woods. My father wanted to navigate the Impala down the icy road slowly, inching over the camelbacks and through the muddy sumps. The Impala had been a demonstrator, and my father had gotten a good deal. It had the chrome package and still smelled of new car. I was not then thinking about our walk on the frozen stream, but waiting for my father to give me a sign. He adjusted the heating vents, which made my feet ache, and said nothing, waiting for the taillights of the truck to disappear entirely into the woods. People who grow up in the country have their own ideas of privacy.

Finally, he pulled the knob for the headlamps and said, "This was a stupid stunt."

"Yes, sir," I said, choking up but also understanding that he was not really angry. *Stupid stunt* was a favorite phrase of his, and I spent a lifetime giving him opportunities to use it. *Going off half-cocked* was another one he liked. I got to hear it that night, as well. But he did not swat me or restrict me or even make me go to bed early. He did not punish me in any way.

Brady was not so lucky. He got a whupping. I was not invited to his house for some weeks. When we finally got to play together, shame kept us from talking about our punishments. He was ashamed that he had been spanked, and I was ashamed that he had been disciplined while I got off scot-free. The topic of the walk became off-limits.

On that long drive home, while my father corkscrewed the car down the road, the windshield wipers slapping away the snow, he and I talked. He was stern enough at first, but he couldn't keep it up. Like other men of his generation, he desired to see some of his passions alive in his son. Men still have this wish, but I think there was something different about it for that generation. Immense forces of history had taken liberties with their lives, and they needed to believe that particular things they loved would endure. My father was happy that I had shown some interest in the woods and the river. He disguised his pleasure, but he could not contain it.

Of course, I failed him. I don't hunt. I don't fish. I don't know any landscape the way he knew the river bottom. All I can claim is that some power lures me out again and again to that creek, to the walk as I remember it, the woods dark and lovely and deep, the snow as white as a page. Did I mention that Brady and I had a rifle? We may have had one. It would have been a .22 or a BB gun. We would have taken turns carrying it. We likely had peanut butter sandwiches in our pockets, wrapped in wax paper. We would have had some in the tree house. Did we remember to eat them?

Writing this essay has also reminded me of one other moment that I had forgotten—or chosen not to remember.

Before Brady's father drove off with his son, he walked over to our car. My father lowered his window. The other man stuck his head inside and eyed me. He said, "This was Brady's idea, wasn't it?"

I understood the ramifications of the question immediately, how it might help my case if I said yes and how it might get Brady whupped. How my saying no might save his hide. Our characters were fiercely loyal, sacrificing themselves each for the other without a thought. There was no question what my character would do. But I felt another, complicating tug. The walk had begun with Brady's chapter. I didn't know the word *plagiarism*, but I felt the terrible weight of it. I did not want to betray my friend, and I did not want to take too much credit for our magnificent, flawed story.

"Tell the truth," my father said.

Which truth? I might have thought.

Ultimately, I nodded and let my friend take his beating.

This essay refers to the following creative works: - 27 -
   The Death of Ivan Ilych by Leo Tolstoy
   "Mercy" by Jean Thompson
   "A Wife of Nashville" by Peter Taylor

PROCESS AND PARADIGM

Process

There is a wonderfully awful moment in Tolstoy's *The Death of Ivan Ilych* wherein Ivan, the judge who prides himself on his ability to evaluate a case strictly on the evidence and ignore all the ancillary human circumstances, finds himself dealing with a doctor who will only talk about Ivan's medical symptoms, who insists on being detached and scientific when Ivan desperately wants recognition of his mortality and the offer of comfort. Ivan's position in a social paradigm has changed.

Recently, I too discovered that my place in a particular paradigm had changed. I discovered myself one night not long ago *participating* in a short story—not reading or writing one (my normal relationships with short fiction), but as a character within a story.

I had made a trip to a major city to give a reading for a fund-raiser, and as it happened, I read with a friend. I won't tell you his name or the name of the city, and I've falsified some of the details. There are people in this story who aren't writers and so, like the innocent, must be protected.

The fund-raiser required that we wear tuxedos, and afterward my friend and I went together to the hotel bar to have a beer and catch up on each other's lives. He and I were about the same age, just beyond the great divide of fifty. "One beer," we agreed and settled on our stools at the far end of a long and empty bar.

This may not sound like a promising opening to a story, and yet writers often look for circumstances like these in the first stage of the writing process. Dressing up characters, either literally or figuratively, in a fashion that makes them uncomfortable or encourages misunderstanding is a productive initial step. These tuxedoed friends in a hotel bar in a strange city are happy to see each other, and after a night of reading their work to wealthy donors, they may be a wee bit full of themselves, and it's likely they have drunk more than a little liquor. They are ripe for consequential action. There is not any obvious conflict and yet one detects instability.

The writing process often begins with instability, not necessarily the dramatic act but the shifting ground. Once the story is set in motion, the writer may simply follow the actions of the characters and see what happens. However, many stories need some kind of catalyst to incite the action.

And so a young woman appears at the bar. She's blonde, attractive, a little drunk, and wanting company. She steps past the long row of empty stools to claim the one next to us. "Can I join you?" she asks. My friend nods politely. I say hi to her, and then my friend and I resume our conversation. But the woman persists. This is often how I know a new story element belongs, even if it seems out of place in the early drafts—it persists. It won't let me shut it out. It demands my attention by providing me with details, which may seem inconsequential at the moment but nonetheless begin to add up.

The young woman offers to buy us a round of drinks. Manly manners require us to decline the offer, insisting that we pay instead. "One beer," we had said, but the hour is not late and my friend and I enjoy each other's company, and now there is masculine duty involved. We will not be responsible for the death of chivalry. My friend orders a round and alters his placement on the stool to permit the young woman entry into our conversation.

She wants to know what we've been doing, which reminds me of another time when I was in a tuxedo and out with a girl, a girl so beautiful that I had trouble looking at her face for more than a moment, as if it were improper for one such as me to witness one such as her in any manner but the furtive. The time was high school and the occasion was one I'd manipulated—nominating her to be queen of the high school's National Honor Society so I could escort her to the annual ball. As a young man, I was crafty in the ways of love. After the ball ended, I drove her downtown, where we walked along the street and stared in the windows of the fading businesses. In the first shadowy spot I touched her arm and she closed her eyes. We kissed, and perhaps I might have won her away from her boyfriend, a college man (i.e., out of town), but two young men, black kids about our age, came by and asked what was going on. "Nothing much," I said, which was true enough, as we were just walking and stealing kisses. I had forgotten that I was in a tuxedo (a pink one, no less) and she was in a gown whose fabric was almost iridescent, as was the smile she bestowed on the dark night, my eager face, and those two young men. And when, a moment later, as I leaned in to kiss her once more and a rock flew past my ear and hit a parked car, I could not name the offense we'd given.

This movement away from the main narrative, the backward glance or sideways reflection, often occurs while writing a story. I always let it enter, give it a chance. Sometimes things that have only the barest of associative connections will pay off in the end. I not only don't know what the connection is going to be, I don't want to know. Not yet. The story will teach me. Figuring it out too early can deform it, so it will merely do some kind of obvious or logical work. Whether it will inform the main thread of the story, I have to be willing to wait and see.

Which takes us back to the hotel bar and us two men telling the young woman about the fund-raiser, and that we are writers and from distant cities and pals. Her hair, I note, has dark roots that divide her sandy skull along the middle part like the asphalt of a desert highway. And in her eyes, some slippage; the tether that unites their parallel movements has frayed a bit—more, it seems to me, than the evening's liquor can explain, but less than one finds in the eyes of the truly mad. This detail locates her in that wide, dim landscape of disconnection useful to fiction. How we separate ourselves from ourselves is a story never too often told.

My friend and I continue to talk about fiction, and she joins in. She has read Gabriel García Márquez and José Saramago, but every third word she speaks is "like," as in, "I love how like García Márquez can like make you feel like like you're really there like." It's a disconcerting combination of a sophisticated topic and an adolescent delivery, and she's desperate to talk. Liquor makes some people lonely, and travel can have the same effect. Hotel bars are often home to people frantic not to spend the night alone in an anonymous bed. My friend and I are overdressed and drinking, and she's overeager and drinking, and we're all a little unstable— tipsy, if you will. This is the kind of situation writers work to create in their fiction. Sometimes in revision, the writer's main job is to make a scene less stable, not to pull the rug out, but to give it a few more wrinkles.

Over the course of the conversation, a few details about her life slip out. She's by herself, visiting from a distant state, but she spent most of her life in that unnamed city where we were at that moment drinking beer. She has two small children by two different men. She has never married. She used to be an artist, making, of all things, wicker sculptures. For some reason, that didn't work out. She takes classes now at a community college in South Dakota. At some point, she agrees with an assertion about literature that neither of us has made.

"Yeah," she says, "that's what like makes a great story—a dark secret in your past."

Chekhov suggests that the writer's job is to distinguish important testimony from the unimportant, and at this point in the conversation, it seemed to me that I should listen closely to this woman's testimony. I began to feel much as I do while working on a story—that rush that tells me I'm on to something. I also felt the uneasiness and dread that accompany the feeling. One often has to step into uncomfortable territory and stubbornly remain there in order to write. This woman's lonely, despairing presence seemed vaguely carnivorous, and that, too, reminded me of writing, when you reach the point where you feel physically in jeopardy.

Slipping the bartender his credit card, my friend pays for all the rounds. He has finished his beer ahead of us, and he turns to me to speak privately. "I can't let you pay," he says, "because of what I'm about to do to you." In a louder voice, he says, "Time for me to hit the sack."

"*No*, no, no," I say, but my friend makes his way out of the bar and to the elevator.

"Well." I quickly gulp the remainder of my beer. "I should be going, too."

"He paid for everything," she says. "I wanted to buy a round. You can let me buy you a beer, can't you? You can let me do that."

I respond, "Will you tell me about the dark secret in your past?"

She says, "I shot a man."

I say, "I could have a beer."

I listened for details. I believe details originally offered to create a sense of place or to convince one of a story's authenticity may accrue power over the course of a narrative and return late in a story in a new, more important role. But the woman in the bar wasn't good with details. Here are the facts she provided. The man she shot was the father of one of her children—her second child, I think, a little girl, three now, or so I imagine. The older child is a boy, who would be five. The man had become despondent. He wanted to die and he had a gun, but he didn't quite have the gumption to shoot himself. He wanted *her* to shoot him.

I'm guessing that she didn't immediately agree to this. I'm guessing he had to convince her. I'm fairly certain liquor was on the scene. As I imagine it, his pleading and crying were getting him nowhere. So he became nasty, dismissive of her. He told her that he had never cared about her, not really, until she finally says, "All right then, I'll like kill you."

Picture the young man standing, his face blotchy from crying, his eyes shut. My image of him includes a ragged beard along his chin and dark stubble on his neck. His T-shirt is discolored with perspiration, an uneven splotch, a ragged continent of sweat marking the front of the shirt. (It must be summer.) The shirt wouldn't be white but colorful, bearing the logo of some restaurant or perhaps there's the image of Pancho Villa and beneath it the quotation, "It is better to die on your feet than to live on your knees."

The young man is indeed on his feet. He has given her the gun. His body shakes slightly, his eyes screwed tight. He has an odor. She's in a halter top and olive shorts, her hair tied back and recently dyed—there is no highway dividing her skull just yet. She holds the gun in one hand, at arm's length. She's never held a gun before, and thinks for a moment about its surprising weight. The noise of the shot is so loud and so ugly, it erases her history.

But she's no marksman. She shoots him in the arm. The young man's despondency leaves him and is replaced by a new and overpowering sensation: *pain.* He wants a hospital, and she takes him.

He does not die. Instead, he presses charges against her for attempted murder.

"You're *kidding* me," I say, but she shakes her head.

"There was a trial and everything," she says.

I want the details: How long had she known him? What did he to say to convince her? Who was watching her children?

Her eyes wander up and down and all over my face. She says, "You're a perv."

I say, "I beg your pardon?"

She drinks her beer and lets on slowly what she means. A bar, a hotel, a man, a woman—why should I have to be told? I haven't been doing my job. I wasn't interested in picking her up, in sharing one of those luxurious and anonymous hotel beds. I only wanted her story. This offends her, and she lets me know that she isn't going to tell me anything else.

"I'm a writer," I remind her.

"You're a man, too, aren't you?" she says (or might have said).

To prove my manhood, I say, "I need to pee."

I get out of there. The restroom is off the lobby, and when I come back through, I see my friend, out of his tuxedo now and standing at the front desk, trapped by the woman. She wants the three of us to go to her room. My friend (who cannot believe his bad luck) came downstairs looking for a package, and she spotted him from the bar. But he slips free again and makes it to the elevator. She turns to me, forgiving me for my trespasses, and the decent thing to do might have been to go with her to her room—not to have sex but to talk with her for a while until she could sleep. However, I was not willing to do it. "Get some sleep," I said, but that wasn't enough. I had to say, "I want to be alone."

It was the truth. I wanted to be alone to piece together the story. When I have a draft of a story and I can tell it's missing something, I look for gaps, for opportunities to step back inside the narrative and make new discoveries.

It was in bed that night, wide-awake and alone in the dark, while going over the story again and again—much like my revision process—that I put the pieces together. The discovery I made started with one simple question about the night she shot him. Where were her children? In her description of her community-college life in South Dakota, she had not mentioned children, and here she was visiting her hometown but staying in a hotel and obviously alone. In our culture, mothers typically get custody of the children—unless something unusual has happened. Her children, I decided, had been with her when she shot the man, sleeping perhaps in another room. Her trial, I decided, had not resulted in a prison sentence, but some kind of probation, and she lost custody of both her children. She could only rarely see them. That's why she was in the hotel. She had flown back and visited her boy, visited her girl. I could only imagine how their fathers and step-mothers treated her, or how it felt to be the mother of children you loved and could not see. She found her way to the hotel bar, and that disconnection I sensed in her was evidence of her battle: one part of her desperate to make someone understand the bizarre circumstances that keep her separated from her children, another part of her wanting no one to know of her shame.

Stories, it seems, often reside in conflicted desires.

What I did that night was put what I knew about her together with what I knew about our social mores, and suddenly the story took off, but it took an investment in both the character and the prevailing social paradigm for that to happen.

However, the story was still not complete. I've been telling the tale from my point of view. That makes me the main character. I had to look for the moment when I was revealed. I circled back to her calling me a *perv* because I wasn't interested in her, and I understood that it wasn't just that I wasn't interested in her body but also that I wasn't interested in her person, not in the blank suffering of a fellow human, but only in what I could steal of her story. This failing by our main character is necessary. The first-person story that shows another's frailties without being self-indicting rarely works.

Here's where I ought to apologize to this woman, but that's not in the job description. The process of writing is sometimes the process of betrayal and owning up to it, and then revising to make the words equal to the task, to make the events carry their weight. Does it make it a better story if I follow her to her room and instead of taking her into my arms, I ask for narrative detail? Then put me in the room. Perhaps we kissed. Perhaps I had my hands on her body when I asked who had been watching her children when she shot her lover. Whatever it takes to make the story work, that's what happened.

And that's my writing process.

Paradigm

Paradigm is just the kind of word I tend to distrust. I don't like the way it smells. Some words have a good honest stink, and while you may not like the odor, you cannot entirely discount its source. But there are words that smell a little bit of many different things— too many things. Paradigm carries a whiff of jargon layered between the unappetizing aroma of pretension and the stench of pseudointellectualism.

Yet I don't think the word is entirely lost.

Defining paradigm is not as easy as you might think. It refers to a perceived pattern or the accepted representation of a pattern, especially if the pattern is an archetype or is used as the basis for a theory. For example, the passage of a person through childhood, adolescence, adulthood, and old age is an archetypal pattern, a paradigm of human maturation. Each stage has certain behaviors associated with it. Acts tolerated during adolescence may not be tolerated during later stages because they do not conform to the way we think about human maturation; such acts flout the paradigm.

From this example, it is easy to see why it has become common to use *paradigm* to refer to the general collection of perceptions, principles, and practices that make up a shared vision of reality for a particular culture. We call this the "cultural paradigm" or the "social paradigm"; specific aspects of it may be called the "power paradigm." When one's practices fall outside the paradigm, one may be seen as operating beyond the boundaries of common sense and perhaps beyond the limits of the law. The term may also refer to perceived sets of patterns within smaller bodies—to any particular set of particulars.

The word owes much of its popularity to the term *paradigm shift*, which is credited to a historian of science named Thomas Kuhn. He uses it in his book *The Structure of Scientific Revolutions*, published in the early 1960s. Scientists meant for *paradigm shift* to refer to a revolutionary change in a specific way of thinking, as in: *The work of Albert Einstein caused a paradigm shift in the field of physics.* Nowadays, the term is used more loosely. It may represent a key change in one's private beliefs or experience, or in the way systems or bureaucracies operate.

I've gone over these definitions because I wish to use *paradigm* in different but related ways.

Within the study of fiction writing, there has long been a loose paradigm for our perception of how a story functions. It goes something like the following: A story is centered on a character with a conflict. This conflict generally should not be imposed from the outside, but should be the product of the character's true nature as it interacts with the fictional world. This world should be persuasively conveyed through sensory detail. The conflict must demand action of the character, and that action should reveal the character. By the story's end, the interaction of character and conflict (in the context of the fictional world) should serve to change the character, and the difference should be shown to the reader and not merely explained.

This paradigm for the literary story is very useful, but we know it doesn't apply to all stories. It is a constructive paradigm, as long as we are mindful of its limitations. The limitation I wish to address right now has to do with the writing process, and I began this essay with a description of my own process to be as specific as possible.

I read a great many stories in draft form every year, and frequently their authors have produced terrific scenes, used effective language, and created lively characters with compelling conflicts; and yet these writers often fail to make the elements come together to create a good story. The draft may work well for ten or so pages but then it flounders and eventually dissipates, or it works well right up to the last scene wherein some traditional redemption mechanism or epiphany tool or language generator is whipped out and put to familiar use.

Why does the writer feel so trapped that she must employ a generic device? I suspect that it often has to do with a limited way of thinking about *story*. Therefore, I wish to present a slightly different way of thinking.

Within the familiar story paradigm, a writer is encouraged to "create a world" for the character to inhabit; the small change I wish to suggest is that the writer create instead a social paradigm in which the character participates. This was the key for me in imagining the story of the woman in the bar. She is a mother of two, yet she does not have custody of either child. She is in her hometown, yet she is staying at a hotel. These things grate against my understanding of our social paradigm. I could, of course, come up with reasonable alternative explanations, but they would not explain her desperate and aggrieved behavior in the bar.

By placing what I saw of her actions and knew of her situation within the larger cultural context, her story—my version of it, anyway—quickly emerged in my imagination. I don't think I could have come up with the story if I'd simply considered her as a character with a conflict.

Let's return now to Tolstoy's *The Death of Ivan Ilych.*

Ivan, we're told, is a man's whose life is "most simple and most ordinary and therefore most terrible." Tolstoy is just that blatant in his argument that the conventional social paradigm is not merely an unacceptable model but is a template for both travesty and tragedy.

Tolstoy makes the reader see and recognize the social paradigm governing Ivan's life and also shows Ivan's rigorous obedience to it. We're told that Ivan Ilych is a decorous man "capable of separating his official duties from his private life." As a judge, he possessed

a method of eliminating all considerations irrelevant to the legal aspect of [a] case, and reducing even the most complicated case to a form in which it would be presented on paper only in its externals, completely excluding his personal opinion of the matter, while above all observing every prescribed formality.

Later in the novella, Ivan comes to realize that marriage is "a very intricate and difficult affair towards which in order to perform one's duty, that is, to lead a decorous life approved of by society, one must adopt a definite attitude just as towards one's official duties."

The story conveys the social paradigm, as Ivan Ilych perceives it, and reveals his proper place within it. But Tolstoy, of course, is ready to wrinkle the rug beneath his feet. The decorous Ivan is injured while decorating his apartment and the injury lingers. He decides to see a doctor:

> There was the usual waiting and the important air assumed by the doctor . . . (resembling that which he himself assumed in court) . . . and the questions which called for answers that were foregone conclusions. . . . The doctor put on just the same air towards him as he himself put on towards an accused person.
>
> The doctor said that so-and-so indicated that there was so-and-so inside the patient, but if the investigation of so-and-so did not confirm this, then he must assume that and that. . . . And so on. To Ivan Ilych only one question was important: was his case serious or not? . . . The doctor ignored that inappropriate question. . . . All this was just what Ivan Ilych had himself brilliantly accomplished a thousand times in dealing with men on trial. The doctor summed up . . . looking over his spectacles triumphantly and even gaily at the accused.

The power paradigm perceived by Ivan Ilych is still in place, but his position in it has changed. He will discover the same about his marriage, and ultimately the entire social paradigm by which he has lived will not just be called into question but abandoned. It's true that Ivan Ilych has a conflict and that this conflict demands action and that by the end of the story the character is changed; however, the conflict concerns how he understands and participates in the world, and so it is more useful to think about the story in terms of his relationship to the social paradigm and how that relationship changes.

Tolstoy's novella deserves more attention, and I will return to it in later essays. My desire here is to show how other stories—less obvious examples—create patterns and use alterations in those patterns to negotiate their conclusions.

In Jean Thompson's story "Mercy," from her celebrated collection *Who Do You Love*, the main character is a cop named Quinn. He is understood by the reader in terms of a series of interactions that define him. The story opens with Quinn pulling his dog away from a possum it has cornered. After describing in detail how ugly the creature is, Thompson writes:

> There was nothing on earth as useless as a possum. But it pleased [Quinn] that it was ugly and useless, and that he had saved it anyway. It was a completely gratuitous act of mercy.

With this opening, Thompson initiates the pattern: Quinn is one who dispenses mercy.

After the possum episode comes an encounter in a convenience store—a damaged and hideous-looking man is caught stealing cat food, and he wets himself when apprehended. Thompson describes the scene as follows:

> The manager and a stock boy had the guy up against a wall at the back of the store, like another sort of possum.

Quinn finds a way to let the man go—another act of mercy for a creature ostensibly as ugly and "worthless" as the possum. Thompson is careful not to have these episodes happen on the same day. In fact, the convenience store trouble is called to mind by the possum incident. This sleight of hand keeps the reader from feeling that the deck is stacked and we're simply tuned in to "mercy day."

Late in his shift, Quinn is called to the house of Bonnie

Livengood and her son Gary, a teenager who has threatened his mother and is tearing up the house. He is another incarnation of ugliness and he's described like some kind of rodent. Quinn has Gary come out to the police car to talk; he does not arrest the boy but tells him to "figure out which fights aren't worth getting into." Then he has Bonnie come to the car. She is exhausted and winds up falling asleep. He lets her sleep. By not arresting the boy and by letting Bonnie sleep, Quinn continues to be merciful.

This episode is followed by a transition so bold and brilliant that I'm going to include it verbatim:

> And that was the inconclusive end of things, at least for that night. Spring arrived, tentative and muddy. Grass emerged from the cold earth. Quinn measured time by shifts and shifts' ends. It was a night in late April when he answered an accident call west of town, on a two-lane country road bordered by farm fields.

Thompson moves the story forward several months to the auto accident in which Gary dies. If Gary were to die in an accident the same week of Quinn's intervention or even the same month, it might seem terribly contrived. However, that Gary eventually dies a violent death seems almost inevitable.

The story has established a pattern of Quinn dispensing mercy, but I'm arguing that it's more than a pattern because it is meant to convey the perceptions, principles, and practices that make up Quinn's vision of the world, and so, I think the term *paradigm* may fairly apply. As the story eventually makes explicit, he does not and cannot see himself as a man in despair, and so he seeks out examples of life that make his own position seem tenable. From this artificially elevated position, he can dispense mercy, which, in turn, reinforces his desire to seek low ground where his misery, in comparison, is nothing.

Thompson reveals all this in small bits that accumulate nicely. For example, Quinn asks for the graveyard shift, knowing that "things heated up after dark, and graveyard was when the bars closed, the drunks drove, and the crazies came out to play." Thompson also makes it explicit that his decision to seek the lowest societal rungs is tied to the demise of his marriage. "Quinn had been on graveyard for four years, since his marriage ended, and there was no reason for him to be home during normal hours. He was used to it by now; it even suited him."

At the accident site, Quinn is powerfully affected, as the following passage demonstrates:

> Quinn said nothing. There was nothing he could have said that would not have been obvious, inadequate. He turned away from the wreckage and the halogen-lit ambulance crews. The sky was blind and black after the lights. The fields were newly planted and bare. The air smelled of gasoline and scorched rubber. He felt angry and unquiet, as he always did when such things happened, at the stupid waste of it all, wasted life, love, grief. He stayed until the ambulances left, and the tow truck fastened the wreck back together with chains and hauled it off, and the road was swept clean of sparkling glass. He was the last one to leave, and he walked back to his car along the shoulder of the dark road. He kept thinking there should be more you could say. Something like prayer but that wouldn't embarrass anyone.

He lingers at this merciless site as long as he can; he feels vacant, he feels dead inside. The story suggests that this is a survival strategy, one that has outlived its usefulness and threatens to become his only way of being, like a creature playing possum long after the threat is gone.

Once he realizes the dead boy is Gary, Quinn starts driving by Bonnie's house and eventually tracks her down at R and K Vacuum Service (that's right, a *vacuum* store). He is as pathetic and undesirable at this store as the shoplifter of cat food was in the convenience store, but Bonnie takes him away from there. Later, in her house, she gives Quinn something tangible to do: stripping Gary's bed and emptying his room. This is Bonnie's second act of mercy. She understands that Quinn is in pain. Much as he did earlier, she's giving him some time to cool out. After Bonnie and Quinn have sex, Quinn—who has been up twenty or so hours—falls asleep, and now it is she who lets him sleep.

Just as Tolstoy changes Ivan Ilych's place from judge to the judged, Thompson switches Quinn's place. Each of his acts of mercy has been turned on its head and replayed. Yet it's not likely the reader has noticed the pattern's mirror image. In fact, having been trained to see his acts as merciful, the reader is probably still thinking that Quinn has sought out Bonnie after her son's death to continue offering mercy, and this coincides with Quinn's own thinking. Neither Quinn nor the reader comprehends what's really going on until later when Quinn, who cannot understand why Bonnie is avoiding him, tracks her down once more. She says, "Christ. I felt sorry for you. You and your sad-sack face and your stupid badge. It was a mercy fuck, OK?" With the rush that accompanies such a revelation, the reader understands that Quinn's place in the paradigm has changed.

I'm aware that I'm pushing the definition of paradigm a little to apply it to the patterns at work in this story. However, I want to use this example because, compared to *The Death of Ivan Ilych* or the story I'm about to discuss, it's a relatively simple and yet wonderfully effective use of paradigm. Moreover, this story couldn't have come about merely from thinking about character and conflict. Thompson creates a pattern and then has it recur but the character's position within the pattern has changed. This narrative strategy permits Thompson to reveal Quinn in a remarkable and surprising fashion.

Peter Taylor's "A Wife of Nashville" is set in the South before and during the Great Depression. On the second page the main character, Helen Ruth Lovell, makes the following statement about

Negroes: "I don't care anything about them any more than you do." The story is about the crucial relationships in Helen Ruth's adult life, those with her husband, her three sons, and her house-keepers. The story is not told in chronological order, but the pro-cession of housekeepers is used to keep the chronology straight for the reader. The story covers many years, from the early part of Helen Ruth's marriage, to the time her children are almost grown.

The family has a series of housekeepers, and these four black women are crucial characters—Jane Blakemore, Carrie, Old Sarah, and Jess McGehee. It's clear that Helen Ruth's attitude toward the servants changes over time, softening, becoming increasingly hu-mane and compassionate, and ultimately something even more than compassionate; meanwhile, her husband and sons do not change at all in their attitudes. You could read this story, then, as one of character and conflict wherein the character changes; that reading is correct but it is beside the point.

The southern social paradigm of that time seems fully em-bodied in the thoughts and customs of the Lovell family. This paradigm is invested in hierarchy and social aristocracy, and it is inflexible, particularly as it relates to race. The story shows Helen Ruth as the intermediary between her white, middle-class fam-ily and their Negro housekeepers. Her relationships with her ser-vants are at the front of the story. The way Helen softens over time would seem tied to her growing understanding of what might have been called at the time "the Negro situation." Again, while this is true, it hardly captures the story of Helen Ruth.

The narrative is too complicated to effectively summarize, but it builds to a moment in which the current housekeeper (Jess McGehee) tells the family a lie about why she is leaving their em-ployment. Helen Ruth knows that she's lying, but rather than call her on it she embraces Jess's fabrication—an act that astonishes her family because it exists outside the accepted paradigm. She tries to explain herself. "My dears," she says to her husband and sons, "don't you see how it was for Jess? How else can they tell us anything when there is such a gulf?" Her husband and sons cannot see it at all. This is beyond what their culture has identified as reasonable.

The southern social paradigm of the time is replete with racial rules, most of them tacit but plenty also chiseled into the law books. Race continues to be such a heated issue in this country that it is almost impossible for the reader to think about the social paradigm the story presents without thinking first and foremost about race. But the paradigm is intricate and the presentation is subtle, and while the focus seems to be on race, the story is actually painting a much more complete picture.

For example, it is also true that in traditional southern families of this time the husband is the head of the family and he has the authority to make decisions for all its members. John R. Lovell is a man of some modest success once he manages to have his own insurance agency. Meanwhile, if you'll excuse the pun, this is very much the kind of thing Helen also desires—her own agency.

Initially, she is particularly rough with the servants whenever one makes a suggestion that is in line with Helen's own desires. When Jane Blakemore says, "Wouldn't it be dandy if me and you clomb in that car one of these weekdays and toured out to Thornton to see all the folks—white and black," she's saying, wouldn't it be nice if we two women had enough authority over our own lives that we could return together to our shared hometown. This statement could even be read as an attempt to bridge that "gulf" between races. Helen Ruth responds immediately with the answer she knows her husband would give, even though she longs to be able to drive and wishes for the freedom that an automobile would provide her. She responds not as a woman who can identify with another woman because they both lack agency, but as a white person who participates in and must uphold the existing social paradigm, which includes the maintenance of that racial gulf. In this context, one sees the title of the story in a new light. She's a wife of Nashville.

While Jean Thompson wants the reader to buy into Quinn's understanding of the world, Peter Taylor knows the reader will distance himself from Helen Ruth's initial racial attitudes, and he uses this to his advantage. This distancing blinds the reader to the fact that her position in the power paradigm is also one that's very much compromised. That Helen Ruth and the servants are on opposite sides of the racial barrier is so evident, it isn't until the final paragraphs that we are reminded that Helen Ruth and the servants are on the same side of the gender divide. (It's no accident that she and her husband have only sons; Peter Taylor needs it to be that way.) In the social paradigm this story presents, Helen does not identify her kinship with the other women until late in the narrative and many years into her adulthood. Listen again to her statement to her family at the end of the story:

> "My dears, don't you see how it was for Jess? How else can they tell us anything when there is such a gulf?" After a moment she said, "How can I make you understand this?"
>
> Her husband and her three sons sat staring at her, their big hands, all so alike, resting on the breakfast table, their faces stamped with identical expressions, not of wonder but of incredulity.

Helen Ruth speaks to them of the racial gulf, and then immediately Peter Taylor permits us to see a second gulf. "How can I make you understand this?" she asks.

When you find yourself with a draft of a story that isn't yet working or isn't all it could be, try a draft in which you don't attempt to imagine the character's world, but attempt instead to imagine the social paradigm that has molded her vision. See if the draft suggests a pattern that you can tease through the story. Ask what the pattern represents. See if there is the opportunity to change the character's position within the paradigm. Do not think that you are to write about the evils of society; rather, consider how *you* think and how you treat the world and the people within it, what social customs you accept without really considering them.

That's ultimately what the story I used to open this essay is about, how I treated that young woman in the bar not as a person but as an opportunity. How I thought being a writer gave me the right. And let's be honest: I've done it again by making the tragedy of her life a comic introduction to this essay. Within this particular social paradigm, I seem to think I can get away with it.

This essay refers to the following creative works:
  "A Good Man Is Hard to Find" by Flannery O'Connor
  For Love by Sue Miller

NARRATIVE SPANDRELS

"Evolution" is our label for the creative method employed by the planet. By means of this method, populations of living things change over generations, and the earth has exploited the process to produce an astonishing diversity of plant and animal life.

Princeton biologists Rosemary and Peter Grant have documented a compelling example of evolution on the Galápagos Islands, where for decades they have studied the ground-dwelling finch on the island Daphne Major. The finch is a seed eater that comes equipped with a conical bill, and the Grants have measured the size of the birds' beaks for numerous generations. In 1977, a drought decimated the plants that produce the tiny seeds favored by the finches, and they could not readily crack open the larger seeds of the drought-resistant plants. Eighty-five percent of the finches on the island died; the surviving 15 percent tended to have larger, thicker beaks than those that perished. Their offspring also have larger beaks, almost 5 percent larger than the norm before the drought.

This change in the finch population is called "adaptation," a frequently misunderstood term that seems to encourage people to think that the surviving finches *adapted* to their environment. The prevailing finches, of course, did not change at all; rather, the fact of their survival, combined with the near extinction of those with smaller beaks, changed the population—an adaptation of the species, not of any individual. That a swing in the natural world "selected for" the birds with larger beaks is the mechanism Charles Darwin labeled *natural selection*. That the population of the next generation is altered, that's evolution.

The most prominent evolutionary theorist just prior to Darwin was Jean-Baptiste Lamarck. He had two essential arguments, both grievously flawed. First, he believed that organisms altered themselves over the course of their lives to meet the demands of a changing environment, passing on the alterations to their offspring. Second, Lamarck believed that if organisms quit using some capacity, they would lose it, and it would be lost to future generations, as well. Examining the giraffe, a Darwinian biologist would suggest that the animal's long neck is an adaptation because it permits the giraffe to nibble from the high leaves of trees, those that other leaf eaters cannot reach, and so, over generations, the long neck was selected for by the environment. Lamarck believed the giraffe achieved its long neck by stretching for the leaves, and then it passed on the trait to its offspring. Examining the finches following the drought, Lamarck would likely have said that the survivors were the ones that learned they needed bigger beaks and successfully strengthened and enlarged them.

Learning is a troublesome term to evolutionary biologists, as it's difficult to separate what's learned from what's inherited. Consider the matter of toddlers "learning" a language. Noam Chomsky long ago postulated that the capacity for language is inborn in humans, and researchers in the decades since have added to the credibility of his assertion. Syntax is a genetic gift, Chomsky argues, a bequest of natural selection, which suggests that what people learn when they acquire language merely has to do with the particularities and tonal variations of the locals. The circuitry of syntax is hardwired in our brains.[1]

------

1. Concerning the relationship between biology and learning, I recommend Michael Gazzaniga's *Nature's Mind: The Biological Roots of Thinking, Emotions,*

If we dismiss learning, then the evolutionary process has to account for every aspect of an organism's existence. It isn't hard to imagine how natural selection has led to most of the obvious attributes of living things, but some organisms display traits that do not appear to be adaptive. Such traits present a conundrum for evolutionary scientists and have led to the creation of exceedingly unlikely adaptation stories. One anthropologist proposed that human sacrifice among the Aztecs was an adaptation because the Aztecs were persistently short of meat. This example comes from a celebrated scientific article by Stephen J. Gould,[2] in which he suggests that such speculation is not good science.

The article bears the unwieldy title "The Spandrels of San Marco and the Panglossian Paradigm: A Critique of the Adaptationist Programme," and in it, Gould points to the dangers of making up adaptive stories to suit an organism's traits, to the undeniable existence of nonadaptive traits in animals, and to the unfortunate willingness of scientists to "atomize" an organism into traits. His primary means of argument is an architectural metaphor. He refers to the "spandrel," which is a by-product of placing rounded arches side by side. The elongated triangular space between the top of one arch and the top of another is a spandrel:

> The great central dome of St Mark's Cathedral in Venice presents in its mosaic design a detailed iconography expressing the mainstays of Christian faith. Three circles of figures radiate out from a central image of Christ. . . . Each circle is divided into quadrants . . . [and] each quadrant meets one of the four spandrels in the arches below the dome. Spandrels . . . are necessary architectural by-products of mounting a dome on rounded arches. Each

------

Sexuality, Language, and Intelligence. Among the many books on the Grants' project is Jonathan Weiner's splendid *The Beak of the Finch.*

------

2. Richard C. Lewontin is the article's second author.

spandrel contains a design admirably fitted into its tapering space. . . .

The design is so elaborate, harmonious and purposeful that we are tempted to view it as the starting point of
any analysis, as the cause in some sense of the surround-
ing architecture. But this would invert the proper path
of analysis. The system begins with an architectural con-
straint: the necessary four spandrels and their tapering
triangular form. They provide a space in which the mosaicists worked.

Gould is arguing that if St. Mark's Cathedral were a living
organism, then the beauty of the mosaic design might lead an
evolutionary biologist to believe that its ornate and intricately pat-
terned mosaic dictated the necessity for spandrels, which, in turn,
rounded the entryways. One can imagine a child's encyclopedia
posing a question about such an organism:

QUESTION: Why does St. Mark's have arching entryways?
ANSWER: The mosaic is believed to attract the worship necessary for the cathedral's survival. This triangular adaptation rounds the entryways into the shape you see.

Gould is suggesting that some traits may have come into being
for purposes other than those for which they are, at present, being
used, and that by-products of a trait may wind up serendipitously
serving a function. The arches are a primary trait of the architecture of St. Mark's, and the spandrels are by-products of the
arches; yet the mosaic so beautifully incorporates the spandrels
as to make them seem primary, as if the arch had been invented
by a testy and demanding mosaicist. Obviously, this example also
serves to criticize the tendency to analyze the part outside of the
whole, and individual traits rather than the entire organism.

Which brings me (at long last) to the writing of fiction: it seems
to me that spandrels are often, if I may borrow Gould's language,

the key to creating an elaborate, harmonious, and purposeful story. While the writer must toil away on the primary structures (those literary arches), in the process she inevitably creates spandrels (by-products), and very often these spandrels come to guide and shape the story, and give the writer the opportunity to create a beautiful and meaningful whole.

If the dome of St. Mark's Cathedral is supported by arches, a story's narrative is typically structured by scenes. The construction of any scene will generate by-products—a lamp that flickers, a passing stranger who comments on the main character's shoes, an incontinent dog, a green light at the end of a dock, a stutter, a tattoo of a spider's web, a pattern in the snow that makes the character think of pitted cheeks. These by-products come into existence to make the scene more vivid and complete, but they may ultimately determine the design of the narrative mosaic to such an extent that they will appear to be the primary units of structure.

Consider Flannery O'Connor's "A Good Man Is Hard to Find" and the introduction of Pitty Sing, the grandmother's cat, into the story. The grandmother, being who she is, sneaks the cat into the car before the family starts their trip. The act embodies the selfishness and self-serving dishonesty of the old woman. Even the cat's name (Pitty Sing, as in the baby-talk expression, "You're such a pitty sing!") and the grandmother's justification for sneaking her on board (that the cat would miss her too much) reveal character. Based on what Flannery O'Connor has said about her writing process, I believe this detail entered the story as a by-product: in the course of inventing the character and the initiating action, O'Connor stumbled upon this feline detail. Later in the story, the cat's escape precipitates the accident that leads to the story's astonishing conclusion.

While writing this essay, I asked other writers about their spandrels. The novelist Steven Schwartz had his own vocabulary for it, talking about background and foreground, and how elements that come into a story as background suddenly shift into the foreground, accruing meaning that he had not anticipated.

Antonya Nelson mentioned a specific detail in a novella, how while writing a scene involving a family in a tornado she came up with the detail of a drinking straw being driven through a cheek and leaving a scar. Scarring, without her realizing it, became a subtext in the work, and remained a subtext until the conclusion, when it moved from background to foreground. In the penultimate scene, a new addition to the family is bitten and scarred by another family member, an action that precipitates the protagonist's final gesture, and in so doing determines the shape of the story.

In a story of mine called "Rain," I put two women in the woods during a rainstorm in search of a lost boy. They were close enough to civilization to hear the rapping gate of a fence, but out of their element enough to lose a shoe in a muddy ravine. Those are the story's spandrels, the gate and the shoe. Not created with thematic or structural intent, they cropped up while I was trying to imagine the scene. In the story's final episode, the women return to the woods, and while I was writing this scene the shoe and then the gate returned and guided me to the story's conclusion. Searching for the reason why she has not been herself since she was last in the wilderness, the protagonist instead finds her lost shoe; this and the sound of the rapping gate lead her into a kind of vision—one I had no idea was coming. I can say without any hesitation that the story would not have come together effectively without those happy accidents, those by-products, those *spandrels.*

Obviously, this process is not an unusual experience. It is the way a great many writers work. What I find striking is the metaphor, provided by Gould, and how it conveys the perverse complexity of the writing process, how it supplies a visual representation of what I had long felt and attempted to describe.

Writing fiction is often (too often) a weird ordeal. The discoveries you must make to write a good story rarely come about in a straightforward fashion. My stock example is this: if you begin a story with the Snoopy cliché "It was a dark and stormy night" and then try to write an opening sentence that is less familiar, you might eventually come up with the following: "Lightning struck the fence post." This is not a cliché, and it conveys that there was a storm, and says something about the setting. It is a much better opening line, and it may also offer a useful by-product, as you now have a charred fence post in your story, which could turn out to be its most important image. This image could alter, or even determine, the final shape of the story.

The importance of spandrels as shaping elements is most apparent in stories written without them. Of course, not all writers work in the same fashion, and any author may work in differing ways from one story to the next; however, I believe that most stories that use consciously imposed details (in lieu of spandrels) fail.

Permit me to prop up the handy straw man once again: Hollywood movies. I saw one recently wherein a woman (played by Jennifer Aniston, if you need a visual) pretends to have a husband in order to get ahead in her conservative workplace. She places his photo on her desk, though he is actually only a casual acquaintance. Circumstances force her to ask the fellow to do some acting in front of her employers, for which she offers to pay him. He stays over with her one night, sleeping on the couch, and he falls in love with her. She also falls for him, but she doesn't realize it until almost too late. They reconcile and the credits roll. It's a slight twist on a very familiar formula.

While he's lying on her couch, she tells him about a watch she used to own that she had loved, a Cinderella watch. Much later in the film, she discovers that he has sent her a present—a Cinderella watch. This gift encourages her to realize that she really does love him. The watch is meant to function as a spandrel: something introduced early on in the context of a scene recurs in a manner that propels the outcome. The Cinderella watch, however, is very clearly *not* a spandrel; it is an obviously planted symbol. The watch does not initially come up as a by-product; rather, the scene has no purpose but to supply an opportunity for the conversation, which, in turn, has no purpose but to plant the idea of the watch in the viewer's head. Any discriminating viewer recognizes this as a phony moment, and the watch's return comes across as a ridiculous contrivance to forcibly compel closure.

One could argue that the character telling her faux husband about the watch is a viable part of the plot. Isn't it, after all, taking place in a scene, and haven't we just been calling scenes the primary conduits of story? Technically, the conversation takes place in a scene, but in terms of function, it's a fake scene—just an excuse, a temporal place, for the planting of the ticking symbol. (The same is true for scenes in stories that are merely holding places for the character's contemplation or philosophical pondering; these actions do not require a scene to exist, and they should not represent the sole function of a scene. The action of any scene should be of some immediate story consequence.) One cannot believe the Cinderella watch is a by-product of the scene because the scene does nothing but introduce (and thereby *point at*) the fact of the lost Cinderella watch.

Scenes that merely plant devices are worse than inconsequential. When there is no narrative urgency, the reader feels cheated and the narrative loses energy. The reader may even recognize the false scene as a setup for eventual metaphor. In the movie, the Cinderella watch is a bogus symbol. The narrative, in its schematic design, is updating the fairy tale, with modern Cinderella being the best worker in the organization but overlooked because of her dress and attitude. There's even a ball scene in which everyone praises her gown. The overt reference to Cinderella (by means of the watch) is like an elbow to the ribs—*"Get it?"*

Sue Miller's novel *For Love* is about a woman spending a summer away from her husband in the house where she was raised, readying the place for its eventual sale. She is separated from her regular life in Chicago, living in a house that literally holds her and her almost-adult son, while figuratively holding her childhood and her years with her brother and mother. The brother will strike up an affair that summer with his long-lost love, who herself has returned to the neighborhood to rethink her marriage. It's a nice premise, complex yet manageable, set off in time and space, and yet embodying the whole of the character's life. Miller also writes beautiful sentences, very clean and precise, punctuated with humor and fine character insights.

However, while I admire most of Miller's work, I was nagged while reading *For Love* by an ongoing disappointment in the story. There was an odd flatness to the narrative. The episode I want to talk about takes place very early in the novel. Because it covers almost five pages, I've edited the passages. It begins with a dental mishap.

> [Lottie] felt a portion of one of her back teeth—an artificial portion, it would turn out—gently slide away from the rest of it. This has happened to her sometimes in nightmares . . . and she had an instant sense of mortal foreboding. *"Damn it!"* she said out loud. She began to shift the food around in her mouth with her tongue, selectively and carefully swallowing until she could extract the renegade piece.

In the pages that follow, there are exchanges between Lottie and her son, as well as a few recollections and the conveyance of information necessary to the reader's understanding of the novel's premise—all written with grace and humor. Miller also uses the bad tooth to convey history and the character's sense of herself, as she does in these (edited) paragraphs:

> There was no reason why this—the tooth—should be so upsetting to her, she told herself.
>
> But it was. . . . Lottie [had] . . . had cancer seven years before. Mostly a bad scare: the doctor was sure they'd gotten it all. But now she took good care of herself. She ate carefully, she ran daily.
>
> She had bad teeth, though, terrible teeth, and from time

to time they reminded her of all she could not now control, of all the things that had been out of control in her past— dental care among them. . . .

What's more, Lottie was upset anyway. She'd barely been holding herself together since her husband's visit the weekend before. . . . They'd fought . . . and neither had called the other since. . . .

And now this. Then she laughed out loud at herself: yes, first my marriage goes, and now my tooth.

Eventually, Lottie goes to the dentist, waits to see him, and is admitted. But the problem is worse than the dentist expected, and he sends her back to the waiting room, where she recalls dental work from her impoverished youth at a clinic full of trainees. Here are the final, unedited paragraphs of the episode:

. . . you waited and waited under the flickering lights with all the other mendicants, hoping you'd get someone who had some minimal competence, who didn't actually seem to like to inflict pain.

Mendicants. Lottie had used the very word in telling the tale more than once, making an amusing, exaggerated story of her life. Today it seemed grimly pathetic. It seemed true. She felt sorry for that girl-Lottie, that Charlotte, who traveled across the city alone to have her terrible mouth fixed in a way that dentists for years to come would shake their heads over.

Late in the afternoon, she stepped out into the rain again and began a slow walk back to her mother's house. Her mouth was benumbed and it tasted of peppermint, yet it still ached. Exactly the way she felt about [her husband], she mused. Numbed, yet still in pain. She was glad for the numbness for the time being, though she wondered when it would hit her—the full sense that it was over, that there didn't seem to be a way for them to stay together. And then she pushed that thought, all these thoughts, aside.

What you may notice here is that after four full pages of buildup in scene, nothing happens. The trip is without story consequence for the character or the reader. It's a fake scene—just a temporal place for the contemplation and explication that go on, and while much of the contemplation is compelling, the reader (*this* reader, anyway) feels oddly cheated at the end of it. The narrative deflates because the rules of compression have been ignored.

The bad tooth does have a function in the overall book (the dentist does poor work and her tooth will be very painful later on), but is there really any reason for the reader to accompany Lottie to the dentist? It seems that the reader is meant to see the trip as consequential merely because it affects the character's well-being—as if Lottie were an actual flesh-and-blood friend.

In terms of naked plot, many scenes in a novel are inconsequential, but the reader should not be aware of this while reading them, or upon finishing them. The reader should feel that everything she's being shown is essential and in the necessary order; this is what creates a sense of urgency in a narrative. The dentist episode fails because the reader feels involved in a setup for eventual metaphor, a scene that serves the needs of the writer at the expense of the reader. It is a literary version of the Cinderella-watch conversation.

The filling Lottie gets is incorrectly sized, and on her spur-of-the-moment drive home, she goes through a great deal of pain until she makes it to her neighborhood and has her dentist fix it, and her husband comfort her. The story in its schematic form suggests that Lottie has returned to the place of her youth to re-birth herself, and the novel carries through with this metaphor, the suggestion being that she cannot love herself or her husband until she has reinvented herself (something her brother, still chasing after his high school love, is conspicuously unable to do), and so she must go through labor and birth. Labor requires pain, and the tooth provides it; it serves the schematic design of the novel, but not the immediate story, which makes it feel imposed. When Lottie has the bad filling removed, Miller writes:

> She is talking now, talking and laughing in shaky joy, trying to explain about the tooth, the trip. "God, what a relief!" she says finally. "I can't believe it. I feel as ecstatic as I did when I gave birth."

Miller may be able to distract some readers from the novel's heavy design, but for me, what makes the narrative flat is that the design seems to have come before the story, and the writer is unable to sufficiently disguise this fact. The tooth business, unlike a spandrel, is a conscious, logical metaphor that fits too neatly in the design, that merely reinforces what's going on, that neither surprises nor adds, that has schematic and thematic relevance at the expense of story, plot, authority, and compression. A spandrel, by definition a by-product, will always be in service of the ongoing story, the at-this-moment scene; that it will ultimately also serve a larger function in the story is what gives it its surprise and its power. That necessitates working from the detail to the discovery, rather than working from the schematic design backward, filling in the gaps in what is essentially an outline.

In college literature classes, English professors often begin the analysis of a novel by talking about the book's symbolic and thematic content. Creative writing courses that discuss the same novels almost never start with these elements, as they are spandrels; and despite their harmonious and purposeful presence, they are by-products and so—for student writers, at least—the wrong place to start. (An extrapolation of this argument will make the following evident: the study of literary theory may confound a young writer because it "inverts the proper path of analysis.")

It may seem that I'm going on at great length about not very much at all. Perhaps it is a small matter, but it can be a crucial one. Often when a writer is stuck in a story, it means that he needs to go back to the beginning and more fully imagine each scene, or maybe simply give the existing material a better read in order to identify the lurking but unused spandrels. If we "listen" to the story we're writing, we may be able to identify whether the material we've written can guide the story to its completion, whether the evolving narrative already has in place the traits that will ensure its survival. Why, after all, should we believe the human creative process to be all that different from the creative process that invented us?

Recognizing opportunities within a story for its mutation into a better story is a crucial step in the development of many writers; for others, this process comes as naturally as breathing, as grasping, as taking suck on a breast—all built-in responses of the human animal. There are evolutionary biologists and scientists in a wide range of disciplines who now believe that many other capacities are inborn, as well. The infant's ability to recognize a face is probably innate, as is the capacity for interpreting facial expressions; our ability to make inferences and interpret feelings is hardwired, and even consciousness itself is the product of selection. A percentage of researchers genuinely believe that humans do not really learn anything ever; rather, we spend our lives discovering inborn capacities. Which is to say, our belief in learning is like Lamarck's naive belief that an organism can alter itself to an environment, can develop a larger beak, can so profoundly stretch its neck that its length becomes programmed in its genes; meanwhile, the evidence suggests that what we know is instead like the fortuitously large-beaked finches, a product of natural selection—albeit, the product of millions of years of selection.

If we don't learn, then we merely discover the range, complexity, and limits of our wiring. Selection zealots predict this knowledge will bring about large changes in our culture, such as the end of psychotherapy; but one of the things it makes me think of is Carl Jung's notion of the collective unconscious, how it seems that humans have powerful, innate responses to certain stimuli, as if from generational residue. Jung, of course, studied mythologies—*stories*, narratives that touch on something intrinsic to being human. And this leads me to think of the automatic writing writers sometimes fall into, wherein all that we seem to be doing is listening to a story as it spins itself out, and the yellow hat on the girl's head in the first paragraph turns out to be important in the ultimate resolution—the spandrels leading to discoveries perhaps because they permit the writer full access to an inborn map of narrative. Could this be why the conclusion of a good story (recalling Flannery O'Connor again) can both surprise us and yet seem inevitable? Perhaps when we talk about the pursuit of truth, as writers often do, we're talking about the ability of the writer to make contact with that pure narrative wiring, to successfully ride the native circuitry.

I know that there are dangers to this evolutionary argument. Racists have long attempted to prove that people of color biologically lack the intellect of whites, and while there is an excellent evolutionary argument to counter this,[3] I am nonetheless certain that this notion of hardwiring will be used by some for pernicious ends.

But it's not all ugly. It suggests that our connections with the past and with each other are more manifold and intimate than we'd imagined. I find at least this one feature rewarding to consider: that we may well be narrative beasts down to our very genes, which means that story has been selected for, that it is in the most profound sense *necessary*, and that the desire for story is a generational longing and so its fulfillment is, in essence, spiritual.

How many times have you heard a writer say that it seemed as if the whole story had been in his head from the beginning? While that might not be exactly right, what could be true is that the narrative structure, that ornate framework of reason and unreason, lies waiting within for us to supply the necessary particulars and

------

3. The separation of *Homo sapiens* into racial groups is too chronologically recent to produce significant differences in higher-order capacities.

tonal variations, so that we mosaicists of the word may occasionally be able to adorn a narrative so elaborately, harmoniously, and purposefully that it will seem that the spandrels and even the cut of the arches are solely of our making, rather than the product of millions of years of selection, rather than one of our truest connections with our ancestors, rather than a secular and exquisitely human embodiment of what we might fairly label the soul.

This essay refers to the following creative works:
    Anna Karenina and *The Death of Ivan Ilych* by Leo Tolstoy
    BUtterfield 8 by John O'Hara
    The Suffering Channel by David Foster Wallace
    Billy Budd, Sailor by Herman Melville

ON OMNISCIENCE

My father said to me, "You like that, don't you?" We were in the living room of our little ranch-style house. I was fourteen and knew exactly what he was talking about. My mother had just brought him a drink, a bourbon and water, and she'd seated herself on his lap to hand it over; they'd kissed briefly before he sent her off. My father was in his favorite chair and I was sitting on the floor. "You like that, don't you?" he said, and I understood that he was talking about female attention, the touch and caress of a woman (in my case, a girl), and he was *right*, profoundly right. I liked to have the attention—especially the physical attention—of girls.

I was not, at the age of fourteen, obsessed with the mystery of sex. That edifice in my understanding was a skyscraper, to be sure, but it was, as yet, unlit. My obsession was with the mystery of *girls*. I didn't dream of having sex with them, but just being *around* them. My friends fancied themselves "leg men" or "breast men," but my interest was more general. My favorite line back then—and this will not only tell you something about my obsession but also (alas) the quality of my wit—my favorite line was, "I like tall girls . . . unless they're short."

I did not spend all my time thinking about girls. I liked baseball and I liked to read. I wanted very much to become a writer or the St. Louis Cardinals' shortstop or someone who knew a few girls. At the age of fourteen, my existence, which had seemed easy to understand just a little earlier, was now full of mystery. I had begun to perceive that life wasn't something that unfurled effortlessly and on a steady roll like a red carpet, the direction, pattern, and texture all defined in advance. In fact, it had occurred to me that one's life did not so much unfurl as unfold, so that every day had a new wrinkle, a novel direction, a suddenly unrecognizable shape.

During this same period, I gave up the books I'd loved as a kid—those reliable chums the Hardy Boys, and the reassuringly repetitive baseball novels with titles such as *Rebel in Right Field* or *The Kid Comes Back.* I had discovered another kind of book altogether. For me, it started with *The Adventures of Huckleberry Finn* and *David Copperfield.* Those books dealt with mysteries that could not be resolved by noticing the time on the smashed pocket watch. I found myself in a new place—the same world as always, and yet not the same—a place that became more mysterious the more I knew about it, and I loved the books that enlarged that sense of mystery.

My father seemed to understand what I was going through. His attentions to my changing intellectual and erotic self were intermittent and sometimes unkind, but they were outrageously accurate. He had been the principal of my elementary school, and then we moved and he taught at my junior high; we moved again, and he taught at my high school. He inevitably knew which girls I was attracted to, what bad crowd I was tempted to join, and which new (invariably hideous) fashion statement I was eager to make.

It is odd to have an omniscient entity in your household. The mystery and tension aren't about whether you'll get away with anything, but when and how you'll get caught. Not that my father was fully omniscient. He didn't know that Bobby Kennedy would be assassinated, he didn't invest in Microsoft or understand that the Kents he smoked would kill him, and he told me on the eve of the 1980 election there was no way a two-bit actor who dyed his hair could ever be elected president of the United States.

It may seem equally odd to have an omniscient entity in your fiction—and especially if one of your goals is to create a half-known world. Omniscience and half-knowledge would seem to be adversarial terms, but it turns out that they're not. Out in what we refer to as the "real world," when people speak of omniscience they're usually talking about an all-knowing deity. When writers use the term, we're talking about a third-person *un*limited point of view, one that may burrow into any available head or heart, articulate things no one in the story could know, access the past or future, make blanket statements about the nature of existence, interpret events, tell the reader how to process the story, judge actions or even condemn them. It sounds similar to a story told by an all-knowing deity, but there are important differences. For example, fiction writers are not deities. We don't mind being treated as such, but the truth is we're merely poseurs. Also, the omniscient point of view is subject to restrictions according to the needs and demands of the story. *Restricted omniscience* sounds contradictory, but really, it's only common sense. Even if the writer were genuinely omniscient, she would have to select what to include and what to omit, whose thoughts to examine and whose to ignore; thus, every omniscient point of view necessarily must be selective and restricted.

An omniscient narrator may be a forceful presence or may be largely invisible, but the reader's experience of the narrator has to be definitive. I'll make that the first of twelve planks in my platform on omniscience.

Plank One: The reader's experience of the omniscient narrator has to be definitive; an erratic or wishy-washy omniscience won't do.

"All happy families are alike," Tolstoy's narrator of *Anna Karenina* famously tells us, but "each unhappy family is unhappy in its own way." To which, I've always had two ready responses: first, *That's not true to my experience.* I've known various kinds of happy families, and a good number of unhappy families that seemed distressingly the same. My second response: *What a magnificent opening line!*

It might be truer to experience to open the novel as follows:

> To the extent that a family may be called "happy" in any sense but the momentary, one may argue that "happy families" have so many traits in common that they are, in certain respects, quite similar; while unhappy families show more variation in the nature and extent of their disquietude.

This narrator seems not at all omniscient but equivocal, pretentious in a scholarly fashion, and possibly worried about a lawsuit.

> *Plank Two: The omniscient narrator's responsibility is not to present the reader with any universal or undeniable truths, but with statements that will be proved true in the world the story creates.*

By saying that all happy families are alike, Tolstoy's narrator puts them beneath his consideration. They're all the same, so why bother with them? The reader does not have to agree with the opinion to be enthralled by the statement. By then engaging only with unhappy families, the world of the novel reinforces the statement of the narrator, and suddenly the narrative takes on the mantle of omniscience.

However, this alone isn't sufficient.

> *Plank Three: The narrator's voice, by means of the way it defines itself as omniscient, must serve to shape the overall narrative; the statements and selections that define the omniscient voice should also define the narrative shape.*

I'll even argue that the definitive point-of-view moment in an omniscient narrative should suggest the overall narrative shape.

Is it possible that the sprawling majesty of *Anna Karenina* is shaped by that first omniscient statement? There are no happy families that get much attention, and the narrator pursues Anna's unhappy family mess, as well as the unhappy and oafishly sincere Levin and his desire for Kitty. To some extent, this shapes the narrative. Moreover, after Anna's family dissolves, the final chapters belong to Levin, who is trying to adjust to married life with Kitty and their infant son. Levin has earlier confessed to having no feelings for the baby, but in the penultimate chapter, he reassesses his feelings:

> "I was disappointed. . . . Not exactly in him, but in my own feeling for him. I had expected more. I had expected some novel pleasant emotion to awaken in me, like a surprise, and instead there was only a sensation of disgust, pity . . . [a]nd . . . far more anxiety . . . than satisfaction. I never knew until to-day . . . how I loved him."

The novel ends with Levin beneath the stars contemplating the souls of all the humans in the world. Here are the last lines of the novel, the omniscient voice having moved so intimately into Levin's consciousness that his thoughts are expressed in the first person:

> "I shall still lose my temper with Ivan the coachman, I shall still embark on useless discussions and express my opinions inopportunely; there will still be the same wall between the sanctuary of my inmost soul and other people, even my wife; I shall probably go on scolding her in my anxiety and repenting of it afterwards; I shall still be as unable to understand with my reason why I pray, and I shall still go on praying—but my life now, my whole life, independently of anything that can happen to me, every minute of it is no longer meaningless as it was before, but has a positive meaning of goodness with which I have the power to invest it."

These last words of the novel come just before Lev returns to his house and his *happy* family, no longer fit subjects for the novel, which has spent close to a thousand pages working its way to this definition of familial happiness.

But many omniscient works avoid grand statements. Must the omniscience still shape them?

> On this Sunday morning in May, this girl who later was to be the cause of a sensation in New York, awoke much too early for her night before. One minute she was asleep, the next she was completely awake and dumped into despair. It was the kind of despair that she had known perhaps two thousand times before, there being 365 mornings in a calendar year. In general the cause of her despair was remorse, two kinds of it: remorse because she knew that whatever she was going to do next would not be any good either.

This voice does not belong to the girl (Gloria Wandrous), yet it's hardly elevated above her. There is a colloquial tone, achieved by its informality and sly humor. John O'Hara in *BUtterfield 8* avoids broad statements about existence, yet the narrator has made assertions that the novel will prove true. Gloria will, indeed, be the cause of a sensation in New York, and the novel will build to that moment and resolve with its enactment.

As omniscient narrators go, O'Hara's has a light touch. Listen to the casual point-of-view movement from one character to another and the intentional comic rhyme:

> He went home late, having gone to nine speakeasies in one block, having been refused admission to two others. He went home without seeing Gloria.
>
> She was spending the evening with Eddie. She went to his apartment and they had dinner at a restaurant, where Eddie ate a lot of spaghetti.

You may not be impressed with that movement from one character to the next—you're not supposed to be. You're not supposed to even notice. But O'Hara has effortlessly transported you across the city. And the city is O'Hara's principal interest, the city with its striations of class and culture, and the way it reflects the larger community of the U.S. during the Great Depression. The omniscient narrator's defining moment occurs halfway through the novel. There are only two things you need to know about this (lengthy) paragraph: none of the people mentioned have appeared before except Gloria and Eddie, and none but these two will recur.

On Monday afternoon an unidentified man jumped in front of a New Lots express in the Fourteenth Street subway station. Mr. Hoover was on time for the usual meeting of his Cabinet. Robert McDermott, a student at Fordham University, was complimented for his talk on the Blessed Virgin at the morning exercises in her honor. A woman named Plotkin, living in the Brownsville section of Brooklyn, decided to leave her husband for good and all. William K. Fenstermacher, the East 149th Street repair man, went all the way to Tremont Avenue to fix a radio for a Mrs. Jones, but there was no Jones at the address given, so he had to go all the way back to the shop, wasting over an hour and a half. Babe Ruth hit a home run into the bleachers near the right field foul line. Grayce Johnson tried to get a job in the chorus of The Band Wagon, a new revue, but was told the show was already in rehearsal. Patrolman John J. Barry, Shield No. 17858, was still on sick call as a result of being kicked in the groin by a young woman Communist in the Union Square demonstration of the preceding Friday. Jerry, a drunk, did not wake up once during the entire afternoon, which he spent in a chair at a West 49th Street speakeasy. Identical twins were delivered to a Mrs. Lachase at the Lying-In Hospital. A Studebaker sedan bumped the spare tire of a Ford coupe at Broadway and Canal Street, and the man driving the Ford punched the Studebaker driver in the mouth. Both men were arrested. Joseph H. Dilwyn, forty-two years old, had all his teeth out by the same dentist he had gone to for twelve years. A woman who shall be nameless took the money her husband had given her to pay the electric bill and bought one of the new Eugenie hats with it. Harry W. Blossom, visiting New York for the first time since the War, fell asleep in the Strand Theatre and missed half the picture. At 3:16 P.M. Mr. Francis F. Tearney, conductor on a Jackson Heights No. 15 Fifth Avenue bus, tipped his cap at St. Patrick's Cathedral. James J. Walker, mayor of the City of New York, had a late lunch at the Hardware Club. A girl using an old curling iron caused a short circuit in the Pan-Hellenic Club. An unidentified man jumped in front of a Bronx Park express in the Mott Avenue subway station. After trying for three days Miss Helen Tate, a typist employed by the New York Life, was able to recall the name of a young man she had met two summers before at a party in Red Bank, N.J. Mr. and Mrs. Harvey L. Fox celebrated their thirtieth wedding anniversary with a luncheon in the Hotel Bossert, Brooklyn. Al Astor, an actor at liberty, woke up thinking it was Tuesday. John Lee, a colored boy, pulled the wings out of a fly in Public School 108. The Caswell Realty Company sold a row of taxpayers in Lexington Avenue to Jack W. Levine for a sum in the neighborhood of $125,000. Gloria Wandrous, after taking a warm bath at home, went to sleep while worrying over what she should do about Mrs. Liggett's mink coat. Eddie Brunner spent the afternoon at Norma Day's apartment, playing the phonograph, especially "The Wind in the Willows," the Rudy Vallée record.

Without overtly guiding the reader, O'Hara's democratic narrator finds the bus driver and the mayor, the president of the

United States and a drowsing drunk, worthy of the same attention. The two suicides—both public and involving city services—have no more purchase than the recollection of a boy's name by a woman in the employ of New York Life. That Gloria and Eddie are O'Hara's primary characters seems almost random. The story engages social class in New York after the stock market collapse, and the blue-collar omniscience is unable to see any difference between the haves and the have-nots, as if the great leveling crash of 1929 were a lesson the narrator alone has learned.

Not all of O'Hara's POV characters are blue-collar folk, but the tone of the novel does not shift to accommodate the upper classes.

Plank Four: The tone of the novel should be set by the omniscient voice and should remain true to it, even when dealing with characters of differing social class and sensibility; this is one of the things that distinguishes omniscience from the serial third person limited.

With O'Hara, we have the light omniscient hand and with Tolstoy, the heavy one. Tolstoy's hand is marvelously heavy in his novella *The Death of Ivan Ilych*, which includes the following line:

Ivan Ilych's life had been most simple and most ordinary and therefore most terrible.

I first read *The Death of Ivan Ilych* as a graduate student at the University of Arizona. Francine Prose was my teacher, and I understood from her passion for the novella that it was a remarkable work, but I remained unmoved. A few years later, I was an assistant professor at Northwestern University and my wife was pregnant and we were having the floors in our condo sanded when I taught the story for the first time (it was in the textbook I was using, so I taught it), and I literally trembled while reading it. The story had not changed, but the reader had. I was ready to hear it, and in the twenty years that have followed I've read it at least thirty times, and each reading leaves me shaken.

That first time I taught it, one of my students suggested that it would be a better story if Tolstoy had returned to the characters with whom he'd begun. Ivan Ilych's colleagues should be reintroduced at the end of the story, he said. Maybe we could rejoin them where they reconvene to play cards. This would create a neat set of bookends, he argued, and wasn't it true that if one has a flashback, one should return to the present time?

I didn't have immediate answers for him, and while I felt some annoyance over a student wishing to workshop Tolstoy, I nonetheless understood that he was raising good questions. Why does Tolstoy use this odd half-frame to introduce the story of Ivan Ilych's life?

The novella opens in a private room within a courthouse; two lawyers discuss a case while a third reads the newspaper. He comes across the announcement of Ivan's death. The narrator then moves into the minds of the men:

> Ivan Ilych had been a colleague of the gentlemen present and was liked by them all. He had been ill for some weeks with an illness said to be incurable. His post had been kept open for him, but there had been conjectures that in case of his death Alexeev might receive his appointment, and that either Vinnikov or Shtabel would succeed Alexeev. So on receiving the news of Ivan Ilych's death the first thought of each of the gentlemen in that private room was of the changes and promotions it might occasion among themselves or their acquaintances.

By beginning this paragraph with the fact that these men had known and liked Ivan Ilych and ending it with their thinking about the possible bureaucratic advances his death provides, the narrator initiates his argument that Ivan Ilych's life was most terrible. Tolstoy writes: "Each one thought or felt, 'Well, he's dead but I'm alive!'"

This opening wryly invites the reader's identification with the men. We're seduced in fiction when it shows us not how people are supposed to act but how they really act. The revelation of their self-interest at a time they should properly feel only grief strikes an honest chord. We've all had moments of hearing the *under*-thought, those insistent and unseemly notions we try to hide, and it's exciting to see one on the page.

We feel that covert excitement again in Peter Ivanovich's uncomfortable time at the funeral, wondering how many times he should bow and cross himself, trying to get free to play cards. We identify with his awkwardness, with the hollowness that may accompany a funeral when your attachment to the dead is tenuous or superficial. We identify with Peter's near-desperate desire to escape all of that and have some fun.

The narrator encourages the reader to become a member of this small community—this group of nonmourners. By wedging the door open in this fashion, he wishes to show the reader that she is a member not just of this small community but of the larger culture—people who want to get ahead in the world, who like to decorate their homes nicely, people who covet material objects, who want to live with a little style, who enjoy the petty power of their positions, who believe they will live forever.

In an earlier draft of the story, Tolstoy did not use omniscience but the first-person point of view. The story was told by one of Ivan Ilych's colleagues and opened as follows:

> It is impossible, absolutely impossible, to live as I have lived, as we all live. I realized that as a result of the death of an acquaintance of mine, Ivan Ilych, and of the diary he left behind.

This opening implies a much more conventional narrative design. It also relies on the contrivance of a diary, and we would have to believe that Ivan Ilych, who led a largely unexamined life, kept a diary even while he was in great pain and up to the very moments of his death. Tolstoy's move from first person to the omniscient point of view reveals greater literary intention. He doesn't want to merely show a colleague of Ivan's rethinking his life as the result of Ivan's death; Tolstoy wants the readers to rethink their lives. Using omniscience, Tolstoy cuts out the middleman. He does not want a character to emerge from the narrative changed but to have the reader herself say, "It is impossible to live as we live."

Tolstoy avoids contrivance by assuming the greater responsibilities and greater difficulties of omniscience. It is the point of view most appropriate when you are writing about a man who is dying and with whom you will stay until the occasion of his death and beyond. Omniscience permits Tolstoy to indict Ivan Ilych and implicate the reader, indicting, as well, the materialistic Russian society of the late nineteenth century and the materialistic cultures of the generations of readers who have since turned to the novella.

Plank Five: Omniscience is particularly suited to narratives that wish to grapple with community values or with cultural mores.

We've seen this in *Anna Karenina,* and it is especially evident in *BUtterfield 8,* which presents Gloria's story as a product of the city, and ultimately the narrative becomes as much the city's story as it is Gloria's. And nowhere is this cultural scrutiny more powerfully manifest than in *The Death of Ivan Ilych.*

Recently, I had another student raise interesting questions about Tolstoy's novella. He wanted to know why stories with omniscient narrators aren't considered coy. If the narrator is omniscient, then isn't he simply withholding information until the end? Moreover, the student continued, how can there be mystery in a story if the narrator is all-knowing?

These are good questions, and especially pertinent to this story, as there is not even the mystery that may be achieved by plot; its title, after all, is *The* Death *of Ivan Ilych* and it opens with the old boy already kaput. Neither the mystery nor the tension in the story comes from whether he'll live or die. It isn't whether he'll get away with anything, but when and how he'll get caught. In fact, I believe that Tolstoy has him dead at the outset to dismiss "escape" as a source of tension. Such trivial issues are tossed aside in order to bore in on the large mysteries that cannot be diminished by the accumulation of clues.

Plank Six: The mystery in fiction with an omniscient narrator does not lie in secrets or withheld information but in the fullest and earliest possible revelation of all relevant detail.

Mystery in good fiction rarely comes from filling in gaping blanks or following any party line; mystery comes from knowing a great deal and still residing in a state of bafflement. The more knowing the narrator is, the greater the opportunity for serious mystery. The closer to true omniscience the writer pushes his narrator, the greater the opportunity for conveying the human state of half-knowledge.

Tolstoy's narrator zips through Ivan's terrible life, telling us what we need to know of his loveless marriage and mindless pursuit of money, status, and possessions. He does not slow down until Ivan begins dying.

Ivan does not feel his death sentence is just, and he makes his best lawyerly arguments against it. When he understands he is losing the case, he does what many accused do: he confesses. "Maybe I did not live as I ought to have done," he thinks. "But how could that be, when I did everything properly?" He withdraws the confession, unable as yet to indict the whole culture, and another round of arguments ensues. Finally he asks, "What if my whole life has really been wrong?"

The novella works to raise the question, "How should one live?" This is the mystery that engages Tolstoy, and it is no small thing.

In a daring fashion, Tolstoy has made the material objects in Ivan Ilych's world attack him and others like him—the ottoman's rebellious springs, the lace of his widow's shawl, and the conspiracy of curtains, ladder, and the knob of the window frame that inflict Ivan's mortal wound. The material world is distracting and deadly, but what then should take its place?

"What *is* the right thing?" Ivan Ilych asks, hours before his death, as he tosses and turns on a couch, racked with pain. No sooner does he ask than his hand comes to rest upon the head of his kneeling son, a boy weeping for his father. Ivan Ilych had not realized the boy was in his private room, until some omniscient power replied to his question by placing his hand upon the answer. His life has been most terrible, but his death provides him with a moment of redemption.

It's hard to think of a better model for omniscience than this story. The opinionated narrator withholds nothing about Ivan's circumstances, making him dead at the outset and narrating through his life from youth.

Plank Seven: An omniscient voice must be opinionated, even if it is reluctant to express the opinions openly; to be omniscient and tell a story and yet have no opinions about the characters, the place, and the circumstances is to be coy.

I've failed to address one of the student's questions: If the narrator is omniscient, then isn't he by definition merely withholding information until the end? A writer always has the job of providing the reader with the necessary facts for the articulation of the narrative. Writers struggle with this release of information, how to convey what is needed while simultaneously igniting the plot. In a story with an omniscient narrator, then, my student seems to be arguing, the release of information simply continues until the omniscient narrator decides the reader knows all she needs to know.

It's a good point. If Tolstoy's narrator can tell us Ivan's life was terrible, he's capable of telling us anything.

Plank Eight: With an omniscient narrator, the narrative is essentially the most economical and artful means of releasing the information the narrator already possesses.

Thinking about this, though, one quickly comes to an extraordinary catch. Unless the story is wholly summarized, then its scenes must justify their existence by being the best or only means of conveying what the narrator wishes to get across. In other words:

Plank Nine: The presence of an omniscient narrator puts additional weight on scenes, demanding that actions speak louder than words, requiring scenes in which the mystery of character is better witnessed than paraphrased or explained.

"You like that, don't you?" my father said to me. He was a year or two younger than I am now, while I was a year or so younger than my own son is at this moment, but I recall when my son was two and standing in the kitchen, and trying to tell his parents what he wanted. "I want that one," he said, his arm at full extension, his finger pointing up.

"You want the ceiling fan?" I asked.

"I think he's hungry," my wife said.

"I want *that* one," my son said.

"Cereal?" I said. "A banana?"

"Get him a drink of water," my wife said.

He furiously refused the water. "I want that *one*," he said, crying now. In another moment he would collapse on the kitchen floor, still insisting, "I want that one!" But before he fell, while my wife and I frantically opened cupboards and drawers, I had a moment to think how the so-called terrible twos are the product of first encountering one's inability to articulate one's desires.

If we'd had a little luck, my wife and I might have stumbled across the thing our two-year-old wanted. But none of us can name the magic box in the secret cupboard that satisfies the residual longing of adult women and men. It is not our job as writers to find the right cupboard, but rather to find the right character and make him so complete as a character that the reader shares his longing for that indefinable thing, and shares, too, his sadness, as his power of yearning continues to outstrip his ability to address it.

David Foster Wallace's novella *The Suffering Channel* is about Skip Atwater, a soft-news reporter for *Style* magazine sent to his native Midwest to cover two stories, one about a man said to defecate art, and the other about a cable channel dedicated solely to images of suffering. The story jumps back and forth between *Style*'s headquarters in the World Trade Center and Atwater's adventures with the artist and the cable station. Eventually, the painfully shy artist is videotaped while sitting on a transparent commode for live transmission over the Suffering Channel. The story ends without revealing whether the shit is successfully excreted in the shape of Marilyn Monroe. The omniscient narrator, however, is fully forthcoming about the offices of *Style*, which will be destroyed the day after the story is scheduled to run in the magazine.

Whether Brint Moltke's work is art or merely poop is the hullabaloo at the center of the story; in the meantime, while the best and brightest purvey shit to the masses, their offices in the World Trade Center are shadowed by the incendiary airplanes of 9/11.

Here, an omniscient narrator uses a historical event to place the actions of the characters in a context—one that the reader can see but the characters cannot.

Plank Ten: Dramatic irony seems especially suited to omniscience, as the all-knowing voice can simply tell the reader things the character cannot know; moreover, as omniscience is particularly appropriate for examining community values, the dramatic irony may have application not simply to an individual but to a community or culture.

Within the narrative of Wallace's novella, New York is contrasted with the Midwest. For example, New Yorker Laura Manderley is described as "slender almost to the point of clinical intervention," while the artist's wife in Indiana is described as "the sexiest morbidly obese woman Atwater had ever seen." This compare and contrast provides much of the structural tension in the novella, and Wallace plays both sides of the fence for laughs. He details the banal, fame-envying Midwest and compares it to the banal, status-enslaved inhabitants of New York. The novel is not merely about the brokers of *Style* who meet their end on September 11 but also about the willing victims of *Style*. Like O'Hara and Tolstoy, Wallace is using omniscience to examine the culture. He presents characters who, like the rest of us, have desires that exist just beyond their ability to articulate them; however, they inhabit a pop-culture world that provides substitute desires that are easily nameable: *Forget metaphysical longing, I wanna be on TV.*

The story embraces the argument that "the medium is the message" but gives it more torque than we can anticipate, using shit as a medium for art, sadistic television as a medium for compassion, and *Style* magazine as a medium for communication. The reader can't help but see all this, and yet she gets caught up in the plot twists, anyway: What's with the empty side of the duplex whose bathroom backs the Moltkes'? Is the poop art a scam? Who sent the FedEx box with the crap art to the World Trade Center offices?

The reader, like the characters, gets caught up in the wrong mystery.

Skip Atwater, whose real name is Virgil and who is tied to both New York and Indiana, is our guide. He's described as follows:

Atwater was a plump diminutive boy faced man who sometimes unconsciously made a waist level fist and moved it up and down in time to his stressed syllables. A small and bell shaped *Style* salaryman, energetic and competent, a team player, unfailingly polite. . . . The word among some of *Style*'s snarkier interns was that Skip Atwater resembled a jockey who had retired young and broken training in a big way. . . . Sensitive about the whole baby face issue, as well as about the size and floridity of his ears, Atwater was unaware of his reputation for wearing nearly identical navy blazer and catalogue slacks ensembles all the time, which happened to be the number one thing that betrayed his Midwest origins to those interns who knew anything about cultural geography.

This paragraph does a lot of work. Note the tone of the narrative voice: a gossipy, almost-tabloid omniscience is appropriate for this story. This paragraph mixes registers cleverly, using contemporary business and cultural clichés ("a team player, unfailingly polite") and combining them with a little yuppie slang ("snarkier interns") and sly humor in the final sentence. Its joke is that Skip's clothing reveals him as midwestern *if you know your cultural geography*. Note that the line is presented as if the voice were not in on the joke. In fact, the narrator presents everything in the novella without irony. Of course, the reader is meant to get the joke and therein lies the irony.

Wallace is a master of tone. He gets away with a lot of easy or low humor (consider, for example, in this story about defecation, how often characters are "moved"). He does it by manipulating tone and mixing registers. Most of us merely divvy up language into high, middle, and low diction; but Wallace sees a myriad of registers, including business diction, hip diction, academic diction, advertising diction, and so on, each with its own high, middle, and low ground. He uses elaborate and ornate constructions associated with high diction and mixes in clichés or operational definitions or outright jargon while describing a topic that one typically associates with low diction; for example, *shit*. The whole of this novella is tangled up in the mixed registers inherent in shit passing for art, and *Style* passing for journalism.

Wallace fans know that he has written about his opposition to irony. Here then is one of his earnest strategies: his omniscient voice works to display the satire while simultaneously refusing to see it. Wallace's narrator does not *get* irony, even as the story is shaped by it. In this way, Wallace's narrator is like O'Hara's, who does not comprehend social class, even as the novel deeply explores the matter.

> *Plank Eleven: Decisions by the author always restrict the breadth of the omniscient voice, but the author may also make decisions on the vertical plane, deciding which aspects of perception the narrator may lack; such decisions will affect the narrative shape.*

Like Tolstoy in *Ivan Ilych*, Wallace wants the reader to identify with a community and then reveal the expense of such identification. The community he presents is the glossy, gossipy pop culture that inundates our daily lives and may even guide the formation of our inmost dreams, and the narrator encourages the reader's identification by misdirecting our attention toward the pulp mysteries of who mailed the crap and what kind of asshole scam is going on with the poop art. We get caught up in the tabloid aspects of the story, making us complicit in the creation of the *Style* world.

The unironic narrator is a crucial element in Wallace's work and the one most often misunderstood by those who imitate him. Their narrators tend to be in on all the gags. The narrator supplies the irony and responds to it ironically, leaving the reader with nothing to do. You don't catch Wallace laughing at his own jokes. Yet neither is his narrator a straight man. The joke I've been referring to suggests that fashion or style is the defining attribute concerning regional differences; put in the light of the 9/11 tragedy, the narrator's unwillingness to get the joke takes on a different meaning altogether. It's as if the narrator is earnestly reporting on the events that led to 9/11, and it's no laughing matter. The voice of the omniscient narrator *is* the message. Here is a defining example:

> The executive intern never brushed her hair after a shower. She just gave her head two or three shakes and let it fall gloriously where it might and turned, slightly, to give Ellen Bactrian the full effect. . . . She had ten weeks to live.

The question that Wallace's novella raises is only slightly different from Tolstoy's. It asks, "How is this any way to live?"

"You like that, don't you?" my father said to me. He was a high school civics teacher who drank too much and smoked too much and spent a lot of time in that big chair of his *brooding*. A few years later, when I was a senior in high school, we would pack up our belongings and shift them to an apartment across town. With my older brother gone and me with one foot out the door (for my high school graduation, my parents gave me a suitcase), my father made a last-ditch effort to free himself of debt. We moved to a cheap apartment and put our little ranch-style house on the market. I spent the spring semester of my senior year seeing all my friends get scholarships while I, who had great test scores and good grades, got nothing. I finally swallowed my pride and called one of the universities. The financial-aid officer said that my scholarship had been returned by the post office marked MOVED, NO FORWARDING ADDRESS.

It seems my father hadn't wanted the bill collectors to know where he was.

Years later, I told this charming family anecdote to a friend, and he replied, "That's a classic alcoholic's story." He was right, of course, but he was also wrong—I felt it in my gut, the instinctive resistance you feel when it's suggested that one of the eternal mysteries of your life is really just A-B-C. I would feel that again when

I found myself the parent of a fifteen-year-old girl, a child so wonderful and reliable that I often marveled at the ease with which she moved through the world. When she took a turn and the things that had pleased her she suddenly found unbearable; when she decided to cut herself off from us and quite literally cut herself; when I found myself at the police station in downtown Houston saying that my daughter and one of her girlfriends had gone to a movie and when I went to pick them up, they were not there; when I told the officer how I had skipped past ticket takers to investigate every theater—it was a complex with twenty-five venues—standing in front of the giant screens and calling her name while images of love and violence played larger than life behind me; when I told the detective that I had driven up and down the wet streets in the rain, that I had phoned every person who knew her; when I told him that she and her friend had been gone now twenty hours; he said, "She's fifteen, right? Smart, social? Typical runaway. She fits the profile."

I knew he was right, and yet I knew he was wrong. I wanted to tell him all he could not know. I wanted to tell him that she fit the profile only if he eliminated almost everything I knew about her, about myself, about our family, about the world.

Seen from the wrong distance, we're all stereotypes. Seen from the wrong distance, none of us is a mystery.

Point of view and distance are intertwined like vision and focus; it is impossible to say much about one without some assumption about the other. In Herman Melville's incomparable and incomparably strange novella *Billy Budd, Sailor,* the narrator presents a story that is distanced first by history, next by having a first-person narrator who does not participate in the events of the story, and finally by the narrator's veiled references to Melville himself.

The story is not a simple one. Billy Budd is a handsome and charismatic innocent, a sailor on a British warship who is falsely charged with mutinous intentions by the depraved master-at-arms, John Claggart. A speech defect keeps Billy from defending himself verbally, so he responds by striking, and thereby killing, his accuser. A trial follows. Captain Vere, who witnessed the incident, reminds the tribunal that martial law is straightforward concerning this act, and the officers reluctantly respond with a guilty verdict. Vere informs Billy of the verdict, of his own heavy hand in the decision, and in this moment they come to love each other. Billy Budd is hanged. His last words are "God bless Captain Vere!" The captain dies not long after, wounded in battle. His last words are "Billy Budd, Billy Budd," spoken without the "accents of remorse."

The novella is set at the end of the eighteenth century, and the time frame for the first-person narrator's presentation of it is at least seventy years later. Its subtitle is important: *An Inside Narrative.* Melville's narrator has the inside story on an event that took place on a ship seven decades before his purported writing of the manuscript. Read the story a dozen times and you won't find evidence that the narrator was actually on the boat; moreover, even if he had been, he could not know all he knows, and he'd have to be a hundred years old at the time of the writing. The voice is true to its first-person facade, full of equivocation and speculation, opinions and suppositions, and a folksy if highly literate tone, as in the following:

> In this matter of writing, resolve as one may to keep to the main road, some bypaths have an enticement not readily to be withstood. I am going to err into such a bypath. If the reader will keep me company I shall be glad. At the least, we can promise ourselves that pleasure which is wickedly said to be in sinning, for a literary sin the divergence will be.

The voice seems old-fashioned and postmodern at the same time, and that, dear reader, is a strategy uniquely Melville's. Oh, it's been copied a great deal since by postmodern writers, but Melville owns the patent.

About Billy Budd, the narrator says, "Of self-consciousness he seemed to have little or none, or about as much as we may reasonably impute to a dog of Saint Bernard's breed." How is it, one might ask, that a first-person narrator can know such a thing about a person he never met? The narrative shows Billy to be a "Handsome Sailor," a type that the narrator implies he knows well, and so it may seem that the narrator is simply describing the type. However, a little later, after pointing to the "one thing amiss in [Billy]" (that he stutters), the narrator adds: "The avowal of such an imperfection in the Handsome Sailor should be evidence not alone that he is not presented as a conventional hero, but also that the story in which he is the main figure is no romance." So then this is not a "romance" but a literary story, which means Billy must exist not as a type but as a specific character. Here, Melville is having his cake and eating it, too, which, I would argue, is one of the defining characteristics of postmodernism, the ability to acknowledge the artifice of the work and yet still pull from the reader the conventional responses we associate with traditional fiction. Also note that Melville is having his narrator tell you how to read the story, a starkly postmodern move.

This novella invents John Barth.

When the narrator describes Claggart, he offers the following: "His portrait I essay, but shall never hit it." Ah, poor Melville, he's just not a good enough writer to find the right words to describe Claggart. Or perhaps he wants to suggest that evil in men cannot be fully explained or understood, that it is a mystery we can never more than half-comprehend.

For *Billy Budd, Sailor,* Melville needs the power of omniscience but he does not want an omniscient voice. He uses the unlikely combination of the first-person reliable-yet-omniscient storyteller to close loopholes and force the reader to make decisions about the story based solely on the narrative and the vicissitudes of his (the reader's) conscience. He provides information that no human could know about another person, but he qualifies what he offers and suggests that some of it is speculation. Melville requires the omniscient insights to position the reader, but he needs the first-person form to distance the narrator from any reckoning. That is to be left to the reader.

Seen from the wrong distance, Billy Budd and John Claggart would be one-dimensional characters, but Melville's bag of distancing tricks permits the reader to see them in their proper mythic light. Unable to speak to Claggart's false accusation, Billy strikes him and Claggart dies. Without the historical distance, this unlikely death from a single blow might distract the narration and derail the story, but the reader is not distracted and instead wonders what Captain Vere should do. Billy is an innocent in all but the technical sense of the law; yet there have been mutinies on other ships and it is wartime. The narrator has balanced the argument at the heart of this dilemma as perfectly as possible, leaving Vere with a difficult and dangerous decision—to stick to the law and execute an innocent, or save the man and risk the ship. Yet Vere, understanding all of the complexities of the event, does not hesitate. "Struck dead by an angel of God!" he says. "Yet the angel must hang!" He orchestrates the trial so that none of the moral questions are deemed relevant, and only the question of whether Billy violated the letter of the law (about which there is no doubt) may be considered.

This act of reduction by Vere seems to diminish the story into a simple tale of what happened, a plot without a story. Lewis Mumford, Melville's most celebrated early biographer, goes as far as to say *"Billy Budd . . .* is not a full-bodied story: . . . what is lacking is an independent and living creation." His mistake is in believing Melville's intention is blatant: "The meaning is so obvious that one shrinks from underlining it." He believes Melville is reconciling himself to the ambiguities of existence, a reading that finds Vere a tragic hero, and this is probably the most popular reading, but there is another widely accepted interpretation that is completely at odds with it.

The scholar Merlin Bowen calls the novella "a study in the

possible consequences of a commitment to a fixed and theoretic pattern." He goes on to say the following:

> [Vere] appears as a uniformed and conscientious servant of "Cain's city" . . . who has abdicated his full humanity. . . . One must admit that there is something deeply pathetic in the spectacle of a man fundamentally good . . . being led by the logic of his assumptions into so false a dilemma. . . . But to go beyond pity . . . and to discover in his collaboration with admitted evil the elements of heroism or philosophic wisdom is surely to . . . slide over the book's many indications of Vere's narrowness and rigidity.

While Bowen may overstate his case, he nonetheless makes a good one. Rigid adherence to a code despite mitigating circumstances is not ordinarily an act to be honored. Certainly Melville casts doubts about the rightness of Vere's decision—members of his crew even question his sanity. Yet to make his argument Bowen must ignore the power of the historical circumstances and dismiss the greatness of Vere's soul.

How did Melville intend for us to take Vere and his decision? He gives us plenty of hints as to how we may judge Vere's act. Billy leaves the *Rights-of-Man* to join the *Bellipotent* (*belli* meaning "war," *potent* meaning "power"). Billy gives up the "rights of man" for the "power of war," which seems straightforward enough in its meaning; however, there is the muddying issue of his having been forced to abandon the *Rights-of-Man,* and even this is complicated by his willingness to go. Furthermore, *The Rights of Man* is the title of Thomas Paine's reply to Edmund Burke's *Reflections on the French Revolution.* Burke was a conservative, whereas Paine was a revolutionary.

These philosophical extremes shed light on the conflict by identifying the range of interpretations of Vere's actions. Burke would likely find Vere a tragic hero, while Paine would almost certainly identify Vere as a villain. It is no surprise that scholars have fallen into similar camps. However, to argue that Melville means for readers to see that Vere is in fact a hero or villain is, I believe, to misunderstand the novella and misinterpret the nature of fiction.

Melville invests this human drama with history, allusions to Christian and Greek mythology, and references to philosophy, social criticism, and cultural phenomena, such as the appearance of Siamese twins in the United States. Like twins, the references seem to come one paired against another—Billy as fallen Adam or transcendent Christ, the harsh lessons of the mutiny at the Nore paired with the charismatic authority of Admiral Nelson, Vere's "madness" as a sign of being misguided or an indication of the suffering he undergoes in order to act properly, the natural regality of Billy paired with the natural depravity of Claggart, the corrupting influence of civilization in Claggart paired with the extraordinary man of culture like Vere.

Mumford and Bowen have very different readings, and the novella seems to argue strongly for both readings, and this is Melville's real intention. He offers a true moral dilemma, in which whatever action Vere takes is both right and wrong, both good and evil. Furthermore, he does not make *Billy Budd, Sailor* into the traditional story of character wherein we see a man faced with a dilemma and watch as his decision reveals him. It is not Vere's judgment of Billy that is central to making this narrative a story, but the reader's judgment of Vere.

Melville balances the scales as much as possible, and then has Vere act, leaving it to the reader to interpret his actions and judge his character. He makes it absolutely clear that Billy is good and innocent and yet guilty, that Claggart is evil and conniving and yet the legal victim. In this light, the readings of both camps are integral to making the work whole; however, the scholars' reasoning grows either from a dismissal of the dilemma or from a study of Melville's life—how he has a history of siding with matters of the heart over matters of the mind, for example. But Melville makes

his case in the text: "Whether Captain Vere, as the surgeon pro-
fessionally and privately surmised, was really the sudden victim of
any degree of aberration, every one must determine for himself by
such light as this narrative may afford."

Those on the right judge Vere to have behaved properly and
see him as a tragic hero, while those on the left believe Vere to have
behaved monstrously. What becomes evident is that the judgments
have more to do with the judges than with the circumstances.
Melville's ultimate interest is not in the character's dilemma but
in the reader's dilemma. The reader must come to terms with
Vere's decision on his own, and the manner he chooses will reveal
him to himself.

*Plank Twelve: The omniscient voice is particularly useful
in stories that mean to make the reader question her life,
stories that wish to cut out the middleman; stories that
intend to raise the large questions about human existence
that cannot be readily resolved, even with the help of an
all-knowing deity; stories that intend to reveal not just the
characters but the reader.*

Melville uses the narrator's first-person limitations to link together what might otherwise seem an awkward structure. Near
the end of the novella, the narrator introduces the final chapters
by saying: "Truth uncompromisingly told will always have its
ragged edges." The penultimate chapter offers a newspaper account of the affair; it condemns Billy and exonerates Claggart,
praising the evil man in a fashion that would do justice to an Ann
Coulter editorial on President Bush. The final chapter is a ballad,
an ode to Billy Budd that makes him into a folk hero, something
like the schmaltzy, deifying songs of Pete Seeger or Paul Robeson.

In this polyphonic ending of ragged edges, the predictable
lies are offered in contrast to the inside narrative, and the novella
suddenly expands to include all of the reader's life. Every newspaper account and popular hero must be called into question, and

the reader is left not simply wondering how to judge the actions of "Starry Vere," but how to find truth in a world of outrageous moral complexity and inveterate public mendacity.

"You like that, don't you?" my father said. And I on the floor, on my knees on the cheap shag, must have nodded. *Girls*—what could be more mysterious and unknowable than *girls*? My father nodded, too, and then he said something that I have never forgotten, something that clearly was a part of the man I knew and yet I had no way to make it fit into the puzzle of him. What he said filled me with a sense of doom, but also with an intuition of the mystery of being, the harsh and splendid mystery of life. Because I knew him, you understand, because I knew him so well, and too, because he knew me, his words resonated then and resonate still, of his own dark soul.

"You like that, don't you?" he said to me. "You'll get your fill of it. You wait and see."

This essay refers to the following creative works: - 91 -
    The World According to Garp by John Irving
    Cold Dog Soup by Stephen Dobyns
    "Good Country People" by Flannery O'Connor
    The Things They Carried by Tim O'Brien

URBAN LEGENDS, PORNOGRAPHY, AND LITERARY FICTION

My wife, Toni, and I meet up with friends at a bar called PMS. It's supposed to be PM'S, but they left out the apostrophe. Toni tells everyone that PMS is a theme bar and that's why the waitresses are brusque. While she's shooting pool, a friend from the university tells a story.

Three women, he says, schoolteachers from Minnesota, go to New York City for the first time. They see museums, shop, eat ethnic food, ogle the tall buildings. Late in the afternoon they head for the hotel elevator with the intention of resting in their rooms before dinner. As the elevator doors close, hands dart in. Brown fingers appear in the rubbery gap, and as if by feat of strength, the great metal doors reopen. Before them appears a big black man, bearded and fierce-looking, wearing a cowboy hat and chained to enormous Dobermans. This brute and his dogs step into the elevator. The doors close behind him. Suddenly the black man commands, *"Sit!"*

The women drop to the floor.

"Heavens!" he says. "Goodness." He, of course, had been instructing his dogs. He helps each woman up from the floor. The dogs lick their trembling hands. He gathers their packages. "Is this your first time in the city?" he asks. He recommends a restaurant. That evening the women go to the restaurant he suggested.

When they ask for the check the waiter brings them a note instead. It says, "Dinner is on me. Thanks for the best laugh of my life. Sincerely, Reggie Jackson."

This ends the story. We return to our beer and games of pool. A week passes. Toni is out of town. The telephone rings. It's my mother calling from Arizona. She has news of many things, and a story to tell.

A woman from Arizona has gone to Vegas for the weekend. She hits the jackpot on the slots—a hundred bucks in nickels. Jackpot winners usually trade in their coins for dollars, but this woman has never won anything in all her life, and she keeps the nickels in the giant plastic cup provided by the casino. She cherishes her Big Gulp of booty, but lugging about her winnings eventually tires her, and she decides to nap. She aims herself for the elevator, but hesitates because two black men step in ahead of her. Not wanting to appear prejudiced, she wraps her arms around her precious vessel and steps in just as the metal doors close.

Immediately one of the black men says, "Hit the *four.*"

The woman drops, the chalice of nickels singing against the elevator's metal floor. The black men quickly kneel and help her to her feet. They diligently retrieve her two thousand nickels. They are courteous and kind. They even leave the elevator to walk her to her room.

"I feel like a such a fool," she says.

"Think nothing of it," they reply.

She sleeps, but before long an insistent knocking wakes her. A bellboy stands at the door with a dozen roses, and wrapped in each bloom, a crisp one hundred dollar bill. The note reads, "Thank you for the best laugh of my life. Sincerely, Eddie Murphy."

I ask my mother where she heard the story. She heard it from her best friend's teenage daughter, who got it from a boy at school, whose mother had gone to Vegas with the woman who won the nickel jackpot.

"I wouldn't have believed it," my mother says, "if she hadn't known the boy."

I let that pass. "Why is it a good story?" I ask.

"It's *funny*," she says, "and it goes to show that even big stars can be *nice*." She asks me then if I remember when we met Elvis Presley back when I was a boy and we were on one of our family driving vacations. It's a story I've told a few hundred times, and I have no trouble remembering it. "There's no star bigger than Elvis," my mother goes on, "and he was *very* nice."

I agree about the King but tell her that the elevator story is apocryphal, that I'd heard a different version only a week earlier. This surprises and annoys her. I understand that annoyance. I hate it when people spoil a good story by pointing out little troubles.

I call my university colleague. He'd heard his version from the provost of a college in Minnesota. She claimed to be a friend of one of the women who went to New York. "It's a good story," my friend says, "because it captures the way Minnesotans behave. There are hardly any blacks in Minnesota, and it shows just how foolish these people can be because they're never around blacks." He's surprised to hear the story is phony. The provost had told it as if it were true.

That night I talk with Toni on the phone and tell her about the stories. "They're urban legends," she says. At that time (not all that long ago), I didn't know what urban legends were. Since then, the term has entered public awareness in a big way. Major Hollywood movies have exploited them, and I've been told that there are some Web sites devoted to them and others dedicated to debunking them. Nonetheless, I still have the (possibly quaint) desire to define the term: an urban legend is a story that gets passed around the country with each region claiming it involves locals. The stories are typically meant to be either grotesque or funny—and sometimes both. They often *feel* naughty, but they're not graphic. The stories are always presented as factually true, and so they will sometimes appear in newspaper accounts. One could argue that they're a kind of folk art.

Everyone has heard a few of them, such as the one about the lady who decides to dry her miniature poodle in the microwave and the dog explodes. Or the one about the elderly couple who cancel a trip to Mexico with friends, but their thoughtful pals come back with a Chihuahua as a gift. The little dog is easy to please because it eats everything and never barks. The couple is delighted until their son comes by and says, "That's no dog. That's a rat." Or how about the couple who go into a Chinese restaurant with their little Chihuahua (this one a genuine canine) and they ask the waiter to keep the dog in the back while they eat. When the meal arrives, they consume it with great relish until they realize the waiter misunderstood and has served them their stir-fried pooch.

I went to the library to hunt down a book Toni suggested. There were several volumes of urban legends, all collected by University of Utah English professor Jan Harold Brunvand. I checked out three: *The Vanishing Hitchhiker, The Choking Doberman,* and *The Baby Train.* I found the elevator story in *The Choking Doberman,* and the Reggie Jackson version turns out to be the classic. Brunvand maintains that the story has appeared in various newspapers around the country. It has been repudiated by Mr. October, but to no avail.

The title story of the collection is also interesting. It goes like this: A woman returns from the grocery and finds her Doberman on the floor, gasping for breath. She lugs the dog to her car and races to the vet. A quick examination shows nothing wrong, except that the dog can barely breathe. The vet performs an emergency tracheotomy, permitting the dog to respire by means of a tube inserted in its neck. The vet keeps the dog for observation and sends the woman home. The phone is ringing when she gets there. It's the vet and he's agitated. "Get out of the house!" he says. "I found what was choking your dog. I extracted two brown fingers from his throat. Get out of there! I'm calling the police." The woman rushes outside, and a squad car soon arrives. A trail of blood leads to the woman's closet, where the cops find a large black man passed out against the wall. Two fingers of one hand are missing.

Dogs, obviously, play a big part in urban legends, as do stereotypes—especially those having to do with race, gender, and ethnicity. The elevator and choking-dog stories both rely on the classic racist fear of black men forcibly taking white women. In fact, Brunvand traces the elevator legend to an earlier version that is overtly racist. A well-dressed white woman steps into an elevator, and just as the doors are closing those ubiquitous brown fingers insert themselves. There are two black men, and as soon as the doors shut, they unzip and urinate on the woman. A related story comes under Brunvand's category of "Restroom Legends." A young boy (almost always white) in a public restroom has his penis cut off by black or Hispanic boys, gang members who must do this as initiation into the group. I recall reading such a story about thirty years ago when I lived in San Diego. According to the newspaper, the event took place somewhere in Balboa Park. Many such mutilations have been reported nationwide, but Professor Brunvand insists they're the stuff of legend.

He also traces the choking Doberman to an earlier tale. A man leaves a dog in charge of a sleeping baby. When he returns, the baby's crib has been overturned, the sheets are covered with blood, and the baby is gone. The dog lies next to the crib, also awash in blood. Beside himself with grief, the man takes the dog outside and shoots it. Upon returning he discovers two things: first, the baby, alive and sleeping in a corner of the room, and second, the body of a badger, its neck chewed open.[1]

Urban legends don't have literary aims or pretensions. They are often about how dumb people can be, how noble the famous can be, how silly and easily threatened women are, the high degree of jeopardy women face unless they have a male protector, or how certain racial or ethnic stereotypes are either exactly right or totally wrong. Poetic justice—that extreme and easy form of

------

1. If you substitute a rat for the badger and add a last-minute stay of execution for the dog, you have the central dramatic episode from Disney's *Lady and the Tramp.*

irony—is a big element in the legends, just as it is something to be avoided (or at least disguised) in serious fiction. Urban legends, in fact, seem antiliterary. Their goals tend to be reinforcing biases and commonly held beliefs.

Yet while I was reading the legends, one literary writer came to mind: John Irving. You'll recall that in Irving's *The World According to Garp,* while the wife is dismissing her lover by giving him a blow job in a parked car, the husband comes rolling home with the kids, playing a goofy coasting-in-the-dark sort of game, and rear-ends the lover's car, resulting in the lover getting his penis bitten off. This sounds just like an urban legend. Consider all the contrivance that goes into orchestrating this dismemberment: the wife and lover have to be performing in the car, which has to be in the driveway, the approaching car must not have its lights on, and the timing must be coincidental and perfect. Consider, too, the extremity of the poetic justice. The excising of the penis or some substitution (such as fingers) is an urban-legend mainstay.

The introduction of such an element into a literary work does at least two things: (1) it stretches the credibility of the story; and (2) it engages the reader in a nonliterary way that can be quite powerful. One might argue that these are the strengths and weaknesses of Irving's fiction, but it's hard to argue that *Garp* is anything but a wonderful novel. Part of the reason Irving gets away with this episode is that it is carefully orchestrated; for example, Garp's habit of coasting up the drive in the dark is introduced much earlier than the accident, and his wife's realization (and relief) that it will take nothing more than a blow job to get rid of her lover is completely convincing. Also, the accident has other—tragic—consequences, and the combination of the absurd and the tragic in one incident creates disquieting resonance. And there's yet another reason Irving makes this episode work, but to explain it requires the introduction of a second novel that uses urban legends.

In Stephen Dobyns's *Cold Dog Soup,* a young man goes to pick up his date (a woman with a hook for one hand) and while he's there, her dog collapses. He tries mouth-to-nose resuscitation, but the dog dies, and he's asked to dispose of it before taking the woman out. He drags the dog down to the street and hails a taxi. The cabbie, a Haitian, says, "Why not sell him?" They then go to various places to sell the carcass—a restaurant, a furrier, and so on. At each place the fellow and the cabbie are on the verge of success, when the main character starts telling a dog tale that's in the vein of urban legends. Each story is so tasteless that even these people who routinely deal in dead canines are offended and the deals fall through. *Cold Dog Soup* is hilarious and it rides on the back of urban legends from beginning to end. Of course, the book is farcical and the reader is not supposed to take the portrayal of events as realism. While *The World According to Garp* is a more realistic novel than *Cold Dog Soup*, it has a strong satirical thrust, and satire, generally speaking, is more accommodating of the improbable than realism.

It would be hard to work an urban legend into a realistic novel, and yet anytime an urban legend is spoken, the teller will insist that it's not merely realistic but factual. No one introduces an urban legend by saying, "This didn't actually happen, but it's a brilliant story." Instead, there will be a chain of connectedness *(I heard it from my best friend's daughter, who got it from a boy at school, whose mother went to Vegas with the woman who won the nickels)* offered as a guarantee of the verity of the incident.

The insistence of *this really happened* is important to urban legends in several ways. For example, you may have been thinking that the choking-Doberman legend is a racist story, but the question is—or at least may *seem*—irrelevant if the story really happened. Is the elevator story featuring the Minnesota school-teachers sexist and biased against folks from the Middle West? It might not seem so if it's a true anecdote about three real women from Bemidji. Is the Vegas version of the elevator story credible? If it really happened, then much of the story's power stems from how this very unlikely episode nonetheless occurred.

This last point warrants scrutiny. As fiction, none of the urban legends would be very shapely. As ersatz nonfiction, they're shaped by the listener's incredulity, the astonishment that such things really do take place. Many of the anecdotes we tell in our day-to-day lives are interesting precisely because they're so improbable and yet they happened. When I moved to New Mexico, on my first day in town, I went to the grocery and as I was checking out, a voice from behind me said, "Pardon me, but aren't you Terry Boswell's brother?" The only person in the entire city I even vaguely knew was buying groceries at the same time, in the same market, and from the same clerk as I. He and I became immediate and lasting friends. I like this anecdote specifically because the coincidence is so implausible. For that same reason, if I were to put the scene into a work of fiction, I'd create a cartful of problems—unless maybe I was creating a world wherein certain things are fated, a fictional reality a step or two away from realism. In any case, the fiction writer who invents coincidences is very different from the nonfiction writer who merely reports them.[2]

A similar logic applies to melodramatic circumstances. For example, I had a friend who called in sick and was fired; her boss did not know that she was missing work because she had been raped the night before, and yet he refused to reinstate her even after he heard what had happened. When my friend tells the story of the rape, she includes the fact that it got her fired, and chins drop. In a short story, the same succession of events might come off as melodramatic—the writer laying on the misery, as if being raped weren't sufficiently dreadful. A mountain of troubles that a real person endures may be compelling simply because it is so hard to believe that such a pile-up could ever happen—and yet it has happened to someone. If the same mountain falls on a fictional character, the work may become melodramatic, or simply *hard to believe.* If fictional actions don't ring true, the writer has to

------

2. There are ways to deal with coincidences in fiction when they can't be avoided, but that's beside the point here. Also, there are novels that *choose* to explore the nature and meaning of coincidence; I'm not attempting to address those works.

make an effort to counter the reader's resistance, and the overall story has to justify the unlikely episode in terms of its shape, plot, thematic motifs, and so on.

Many good and great novels have improbable plots or premises (*Moby Dick* comes to mind), but while the memoirist's job would be to convince the reader that such and such really happened, the fiction writer's job is to convince the reader that the unlikely episode is a legitimate part of the world the novel represents. The real world may hand out torture to innocents, sudden illness to heroes, and utterly random death to anyone; and the nonfiction writer may report these events without having to justify their existence (their *inclusion*, perhaps, but not their existence). However, the fiction writer invents his world, and the justification for every action must be built into the narrative.

Once urban legends are labeled "fiction," the same incredulity that has fed them now works against them. In a work of fiction, such incredulity encourages a reader to toss a partially read book onto the recycling pile, no longer willing to suspend disbelief. In all of the recent controversy over fiction being packaged as memoir (most recently, James Frey's ersatz memoir *A Million Little Pieces*), there has been little talk about the differing demands of the genres. Creative nonfiction probably has an equal number of demands as fiction, but they're *different* demands. There's a real difference between experiencing the unlikely and inventing it— something like the difference between telling an anecdote about having met a very affable Elvis, and telling a fictional story in which you pretend you've met him. No matter how friendly you make the King, if you're making it up, it does not reveal him.

Let's consider what we would have to do to convert an urban legend into a literary short story. I want to use the elevator story. I prefer the Vegas version because I like the bucket of coins and how they spill on the elevator floor. I like hearing the coins sing.

The first thing I'd do is make the point-of-view character one of the black men, no longer a celebrity. I'd make the second man his son. It's his son who says, "Hit the *four*," just to see what the white woman will do. He says it so fiercely that his father almost drops to the floor with her. Instead, he helps the woman up, kneels to collect her nickels, as does his son, who is now overly friendly and conciliatory. The father does not want her to see that they are *not* staying on the fourth floor, and so he and his son get off with her and walk her to her room. "I feel like a fool," she says. As soon as the door closes, the son begins laughing. The father ushers his son down the hotel corridor. He is intensely disturbed, in part because of his son's aggression, in part by the woman's humiliation, and in part by his own confused feelings, as he cannot deny that he found a measure of satisfaction in seeing the white woman fall.

This could be material at the heart of a literary story. It makes the events the result of motivated action rather than contrived coincidence. It makes the relationships among the characters multifaceted. It substitutes familial connections for celebrity. It moves the center of the story away from the surface event and into the inner life of the main character. Rather than blithely ridicule the woman, the story would attempt to investigate the real and gnarly interplay among familial loyalty, good intentions, malevolence, racial fear, and sexual politics. Not that it would attempt this by means of a calculated journey through each issue; rather, it would engage these subjects through the investigation of this character's complex responses.

Flannery O'Connor does something like this in "Good Country People," and for that matter, in many of her stories. The plot of "Good Country People" reads like an urban legend or a joke about the farmer's daughter. A traveling salesman comes to the rural South and works to seduce a country girl, who in this case has a Ph.D. and an artificial leg, but once he gets her in the loft and presumably ready to make hay, he instead takes her wooden leg and skedaddles. The taking of the leg is what makes the story astonishing, and that act is clearly in urban legend territory. O'Connor talks about the story in *Mystery and Manners*:

I'll admit that, paraphrased in this way, the situation is simply a low joke. The average reader is pleased to observe anybody's wooden leg being stolen. But without ceasing to appeal to him and without making any statements of high intention, this story does manage to operate at another level of experience, by letting the wooden leg accumulate meaning. Early in the story we're presented with the fact that the Ph.D. is spiritually as well as physically crippled. She believes in nothing but her own belief in nothing, and we perceive that there is a wooden part of her soul that corresponds to her wooden leg. . . . And when the Bible salesman steals it, the reader realizes that he has taken away part of the girl's personality and has revealed her deeper affliction to her for the first time.

It would seem that O'Connor has offered the key to using urban legends in literary fiction: the story must also "operate at another level of experience."

My mother liked the elevator story because it involved a celebrity doing what she saw as a nice thing, and (as she puts it) the story *tickled* her. My university colleague was more specific in his reason for liking the story: it illustrates his politics, how racial ignorance spawns fear. A danger of embracing a story because it supports your political beliefs is that it can lead you to accept things of dubious origin and cause you to overlook details that you would otherwise question. The story, after all, depends on contrivance, one-dimensional characters, and stereotypes. By showing the black man as wealthy and able to bestow generosity that is not merely humanitarian but also monetary, it buys into another corrupt belief system, one wherein the wealthy are, by definition, more generous and intelligent than others. And so the ultimate proof of the black man's superiority is that he can be nice to the women face-to-face and then get away with expressing his contempt by providing them with presents. The story buys into sexist stereotypes as well: the white fool in almost all versions of this story is a woman.

But what if it really did happen? What if you were in that elevator with Eddie Murphy and you saw the woman drop to the floor, the shiny nickels flying about? If it were me, I'd help her out, along with my new buddy Ed, and when she was safely gone, I'd laugh, too. The truth is that almost any of us would laugh as long as she dropped to the floor and we didn't. The feeling of superiority is one of the prime motivations for laughter; and make no mistake about it, a large part of the reason I'm laughing is because that fool was exposed as a racist while my attitudes, whatever they may be, are still hidden. This is also why this story, which is ostensibly politically correct, comes off as racist. Its deepest appeal requires the degradation of the fool to elevate the listener, whose prejudices remain unexposed, and who can feel superior and okay, that his racial attitudes are fine in comparison to the ditz who winds up on her butt.

Humor theorists speculate that the three main sources of comedy are feelings of superiority, recognitions of incongruity, and feelings of relief. As long as an urban legend is believed to be a true event, all three of these factors may be working. There's a brand of humor in the popular media that replicates the urban-legend stance—a mock-reality approach to comedy made popular most recently by Sacha Baron Cohen in the HBO program *Da Ali G Show* and in the *Borat* movie. His fictional personae interact with real people who assume that Cohen's characters should be taken seriously. (Some of the people are even celebrities!) The viewing audience is in on the joke, but the victims are not. The viewer is not asked to believe in the fictional character but in the unlikely event—such as a man getting a group of real people in an actual Arizona bar to sing along with "Throw the Jew Down the Well." Incredulity shapes the mininarratives, and the tension in some of the episodes is extreme and uncomfortable, as Cohen's character pushes the dupes further and further into humiliating territory. If there's any question about the authenticity of the dupes (as there seems to be in parts of the movie), it dampens the humor.[3] The bits are about just how dumb people can be, how gullible the famous can be, how uncomfortable we are with awkward foreigners and inappropriate comments, and so on. Cohen creates a live version of urban legends, and he's often extraordinarily funny. Typically, the darker and less acceptable the episodes become, the more they make us laugh. Polite humor, after all, rarely evokes more than a smile.

Does similar logic (I'm making a leap here) apply to erotica?

I once attended a lecture about pornography in day-to-day life. A professor of English argued that a big percentage of what we're sold in advertising and by means of film and other conduits of popular culture is pornographic, not because it is sexually graphic but because it is insistently unbalanced in its depictions of men and women. She defined pornography as the portrayal of sexual partners in unequal relationships, and she had a lengthy slide show of images from magazine and television commercials, as well as stills from popular films, that showed men in dominating physical positions in relation to the women in the same shots. She argued that pornography has less to do with sex than with feelings of superiority based on gender, and that pop culture is rife with the stuff. She argued in favor of true erotica—sexual material with genuinely equal partners—saying that we need to promote true erotica to provide an outlet for sexual curiosity that is not pornographic.

I was interested in this suggestion, but when a member of the audience asked for examples of genuine erotica in popular culture, she could provide *none*—except those that had no sexual content whatsoever. She showed movie clips of women standing up to men, but there were no examples of men and women having a balanced sexual relationship.

------

3. If Cohen's character is not in a real bar in Arizona but a studio with actors who follow a written script in singing "Throw the Jew Down the Well," most of the humor is lost.

Is it possible that politically correct sex just isn't that sexy?

I raised my hand to ask if she knew of examples of such erotica in literature. She named a novel in which a marriage of twenty years is portrayed and the spouses are equal partners. A voice from the back of the room asked, "Is there any sex in it?" She made a face. No, there wasn't any sex. Even in the lesbian sexual material she studied there was a great deal of role playing with unequal partners, such as women dressed as cops with billy clubs—all the kinds of things you might see in heterosexual pornography.

Portraying sex between utterly equal and loving partners is a lot like having a story without any conflict—it's *dull*. All that's left is the most banal of motivations: to see people naked, to witness part A intersecting with part B. Without conflict, there's no tension and no justification within a story to have such a scene because it fails to reveal character. A sex scene between equal partners is gratuitous because there's nothing to justify its existence but the barest kind of titillation.

So what am I getting at?

I'm suggesting that many of the urban legends are a kind of minor-league pornography, and they're passed like dirty jokes around the country. The tellers and listeners (I count myself among them) get the same sort of grubby thrill from these stories as from obscene pictures, but the experience *seems* cleaner because we can deny the ugliness of the thrill through the teller's insistence that *this really happened,* and all we're doing is listening to (and later repeating) a factual report of a weird occurrence. The tales have to be presented as true stories because fiction cannot rely on the assurance of *this really happened.*

Or can it?

Some works of fiction aggressively tangle with the issue of *this really happened,* and none more successfully than Tim O'Brien's *The Things They Carried,* a book of interconnected stories that chronicles the Vietnam experience. O'Brien does not call the book a novel or a story collection or a story cycle, but simply "a work of fiction." The book embraces (and the stories embody) the argument that as soon as any war tale takes on a recognizable narrative shape it becomes a lie. War is chaos and incoherence, O'Brien argues, while narratives are shapely and powerfully coherent. Thus, he gives himself the task of conveying stories that do not look like stories.

The title story has as its narrative shape a list of the things soldiers carry, and a later story reads like a "how-to" essay. All of the stories that are set in Vietnam have nonnarrative shapes, except the ones that are overtly implausible. (In "Sweetheart of the Song Tra Bong," a girl visits her boyfriend while he's in the jungle in Vietnam, and she winds up going out on secret missions.) To further complicate the relationship between fact and fiction, O'Brien dedicates the book to its characters, and one of the characters is named Tim O'Brien. However, the book is not aiming to seduce you into believing that the fiction really happened; rather, the book is trying to make you question the reality of all reports—fictional and otherwise—about the Vietnam War or any war.

In a chapter called "How to Tell a True War Story," the narrator pulls out that old war chestnut of a grunt falling on a live grenade to save his buddies. The narrator then argues that this story—a war legend—is a lie even if it really happened. One might argue that the same is true about many urban legends; they insist on a lie, even if the example they present really were to be "true."

It is a widely held misconception that "art" is one facet of the larger entertainment industry. In terms of its aims, art is essentially the opposite of entertainments. Entertainments include not just urban legends but all of the junk genres of pop culture: TV shows, Hollywood films, pop novels, and so on. These works tend to reinforce the biases and prejudices of the audience, encouraging the audience to believe they're just fine the way they are. (Hollywood's term for this is "a feel-good movie.") But art—all art—has to work to alter the vision of its audience. I'm not saying that there aren't occasions when entertainments transcend their aim and become art, and I'm certainly not suggesting that art must not entertain, but the ultimate aim of an entertainment is to confirm the reader's existing sense of how things are and how things should be, while the aim of the literary artist is to upset and disrupt that vision.

Does this relationship hold up for the connection between pornography and erotic art? I think it might. Pornography is not merely steeped in the graphic, it is defined by it: porn is generally defined as "sexually explicit materials." No porn that I've ever seen or heard about has any legitimate interest in character development or most of the other literary aspects of narrative. And the difference between hard-core and soft-core porn is the visual guarantee that the actors are literally having sex and not pretending; in other words, they assure the viewer *this really happened*. And that, as I see it, is what's most offensive about pornography—the "lie" of *this really happened*.

I don't mean to discount the potentially damaging influence of pornography on the lives of the actors who perform in the films or on stage—and yet I'm going to. My interest is in the power of the work on its readers or viewers, and it's an error, I think, to say that viewing people having sex is inherently offensive, and ultimately that's what most porn arguments boil down to. Frankly, that just doesn't make sense. But I still find pornography offensive because while the intercourse is physically actual, it's a lie, and the whole narrative exists only for that (physically actual) lie.

Oh, there are plenty of reasons to be offended by pornography, but don't dismiss this one. Fictions that use the promise of *this really happened* to function are not merely meretricious, they're downright treacherous. They undercut true stories and genuine feelings and motivations. They encourage phony beliefs. They provide fodder for hacks (particularly, of late, AM radio hacks) and hack politicians, especially in smear campaigns (think Swift Boat). They are the stuff of dictators, but they are not the exclusive property of the powerful. I just read about a six-year-old girl who entered an essay contest with the prize of tickets to a Hannah Montana concert, and the girl (with her mother's help and guidance) began the essay by saying that her father had died in Iraq over the summer. Only after she'd been awarded first place did the committee discover that her father was not a soldier and had not died in Iraq.

It's fitting, I guess, that John Bobbitt, the man who had his penis cut off by his wife and sewn back on by doctors—the man to whom an urban legend really *did* happen—has gone on to become a porno star. His appeal, I've been told, is that people wish to see his "Frankenstein cock" in action. Porn trivializes real sexual relationships by using the assurance of *this really happened* in place of the necessary elements of story and character.

Fictions that assure their audience *this really happened* are obscene—the type, like urban legends, that pretends to be factual, and the type, like pornography, that uses the literal in place of the imaginative.

No work of serious fiction relies on such assurance. The fiction writer's obligation is to do the opposite. Declare your work as fiction. Doing so forces you to take responsibility for the imaginary worlds you create, to fully imagine them, to fully investigate them, to explore all the possibilities of character, and to construct stories that mean something precisely because they never happened. They matter because they come together in a carefully crafted manner to touch on something essential and true about the way we live.

Housekeeping by Marilynne Robinson
The Left Hand of Darkness by Ursula K. Le Guin
"Labor Day Dinner" and "Friend of My Youth" by Alice Munro
"In the Gloaming" by Alice Elliott Dark
"Indian Camp" by Ernest Hemingway

THE ALTERNATE UNIVERSE

There is a moment in Marilynne Robinson's novel *Housekeeping* in which a girl and a woman find themselves in a boat on a lake in the dark of night. The lake is bisected by a railroad bridge. Years earlier a train derailed on this bridge, purling into the water and disappearing. They are suspended by means of the water above the lost train, while, suspended above them on the bridge, another train approaches.

> We had ridden in against the bridge . . . when the girders began to hum. She rested the flat of her hand against a piling. The sound grew louder and louder, and there was a trembling through the whole frame. The whole long bridge was as quick and tense as vertebrae, singing with one alarm. . . . Then the bridge began to rumble and shake as if it would fall. Shock banged and pounded in every joint. I saw a light pass over my head like a meteor, and then I smelled hot, foul, black oil and heard the gnash of wheels along the rails. It was a very long train.

When people talk about magical moments in fiction, I suspect that they mean episodes like this one. It is unforgettable. I don't know that such magic can be taught, but I'll offer a strategy, a simple metaphor that might permit a writer to return to those stories that aren't all they could be, the stories that may be well crafted but lack magic. Most of us tend to have a drawer full of such stories. The strategy is necessarily simple. If you can approach complex matters by complex means, you probably don't need to read this essay. It's aimed at those of you who are like me and must find a simple path and hope it leads to an interesting place.

My understanding of the alternate universe started with comic books. The first one I remember was in *Superman.* The alternate universe was just like our world only everything was backward. People walked backward, cars drove backward, people aged backward, and when their speech appeared in their voice balloons, it was typed backward, so that "Hi" was "Ih," and "Superman" was "Namrepus." Even as a child, I could see this was lame. But the *idea* of an alternate universe interested me, and it would turn up in comics—and elsewhere—time and again. Superman's alternate universe was called Bizarro World, and you may recall the *Seinfeld* episode in which Elaine encounters Bizarro Jerry and Kramer and George, who are kind and ethical and humorless.

Often the alternate world exists in a different dimension. I never knew exactly what that meant, but I pictured it as something like a double exposure, so that our world and the alternate world coexisted in the same space but we could only experience the other world under special circumstances. In a comic I only vaguely remember, Lois Lane finds a shimmering bit of air and when she steps into it, she enters an alternate universe. There she meets another Lois Lane, who is just like her except that *she* has married Clark Kent. The alternate Clark and Lois have two or three Superkids flying around in the basement. When Lois finds her way back to our universe, she gets a kick out of describing the place to Clark Kent. "Ha, ha," she says, "in that other world *you* were secretly Superman." He laughs, too, all the while showing that sly little smile of his.

It's easy to see why the notion of an alternate universe is appealing. It indulges the "what if" syndrome. But there is another appeal, a more compelling one: there are times when it seems like there *must* be some other way of living, moments when the utterly ordinary takes on a measure of strangeness. Now and again, you may even feel as if you live in two worlds at once, one that is orderly and regular and looks like the representations of life you're accustomed to, and another that is disorderly and irregular and nothing like representations you've seen anywhere.

It's rare for serious writers to create alternate worlds that are literal, but of course there's Alice and her looking glass and there's plenty of science fiction. In Ursula K. Le Guin's *The Left Hand of Darkness,* the alternate universe is literally another planet in another solar system. An Earthling is sent to bring this planet into the federation—to make it a part of *our* universe. He finds people like himself with one important exception: they have no sex parts. There are no men or women, just people. Once every few weeks, a person goes into *kemmer,* which is something like an animal going into heat. During that period, the person develops genitalia. One time it may be male genitalia, and the next time, female genitalia. Le Guin wishes to present a world without sex roles to make us understand the power they have on our own planet. The Earthling, because he packs his genitals on him all of the time, is considered a pervert.

There are other exceptions, but most times when the alternate world is made literal, the reading experience is no more rewarding than when comic-book characters do things backward. Such stories tend to be merely about the ideas or the politics that form the premise. Or they're adventure stories, and they're primarily about the plot. Sometimes they work as literature but not often. The literary writer is more likely to find an alternate world residing within this world. He dives into the character's vision of the world in order to discover the moments when that vision expands beyond its usual limits.

Many stories have the suggestion of two worlds existing at once. We may call them the world of the intellect and the world of the heart, the physical world and the world of the mind, but any label we provide limits them in possibly fatal ways. If I were to make a list of what it takes to show a character witnessing something of another world, I'd start by saying that the worlds should not be consciously constructed to represent ideas or ideals. I would argue that the shimmer that permits the character entry needs to have some kind of concrete embodiment, and at the same time, this shimmer (or bridge) must exceed its physical definition. Finally, the reader should experience this moment of passage viscerally.

Alice Munro's "Labor Day Dinner" opens with George and Roberta and Roberta's daughters crossing the lawn to Valerie's house. Each carries something—lawn chairs, bottles of wine, and a raspberry bombe. (It's always good to have some kind of *bomb* in the opening of a story.) Munro writes, "These four people are costumed in a way that would suggest they were going to different dinner parties." Munro describes their attire and then the narrative pivots, moving backward in time to let us know that they made the short drive to Valerie's over back roads in a pickup—the girls in the bed on lawn chairs. The narrative continues moving backward and into the cab of the truck, where Roberta is feeling that George hates her, which is making her crazy. The narrative moves back to before the drive, to their bedroom. Roberta asks about her halter top, and George says, "Your armpits are flabby." This brief conversation is another pivot point, as the scene then reverses its movement and we return to the truck that is heading toward Valerie's house.

The next section starts up just slightly ahead of where the first one began. They're still crossing the yard. The scene moves forward to introduce Valerie, her children, and her son David's girlfriend, Kimberly. As soon as the last is introduced, the scene pivots backward. For the remainder of the section Munro provides the backstory of how this crew came together, especially how Roberta and George met through Valerie.

The next section again starts only slightly ahead of where the previous one opened. Once more, the narrative movement edges forward a tiny bit, and then pivots and moves into background material. It is as if the narrative movement itself is insisting on the difficulty of arriving anywhere, just how much luggage one is always dragging along, how precarious the journey may be, how even people going to the same location are still heading toward different destinations, and how much preparation is required for any kind of forward movement—even if much of the preparation is useless or destructive or just for show.

Once all eight characters have been introduced, the story makes its most ambitious forward movement yet. The girls look for a costume, George goes out to cut the grass with a scythe, and Roberta and Valerie begin talking. The back-and-forth movement is more complicated in this section, but there are still pivot points and contradictory chronological movements. At one point, Roberta, talking about her troubles, says to Valerie, "It's not the house, it's not the children. It's just something black that rises." Valerie responds, "Oh, there's always something black."

The story is impressive for its handling of point of view and its ability to move seamlessly backward and forward in time without disrupting the narrative's forward momentum, but what makes this story remarkable is that the "something black that rises" will be given a literal presence. There are other indirect references to it, including the recitation of "Here comes a candle to light you to bed. Here comes a chopper to chop off your head." Keep in mind that George is *scything*, while Roberta, you'll recall, is lugging a bomb. And later dull David compares their dinner party to "the Incas eating off gold plates while Pizarro was landing on the coast."

The story is not just a contemplation of ruin, but an acknowledgment that it is inevitable and that there may be a wish, which surfaces now and again, to just get on with it and let that darkness come—even to whistle for its arrival.

"A gibbous moon," George notes as they drive away, and Roberta understands this comment is an offer of partial reconciliation, but she believes her best course is to act indifferent, which she understands is attractive. A lot of writers would have ended here. The characters have come full circle in the drive, and Roberta's feelings have come full circle—from feeling crazy to acting indifferent and in charge. But Munro introduces a "dark-green 1969 Dodge . . . travelling at between eighty and ninety miles an hour." The driver is a drunken young man, who has forgotten the headlights. He sees the road by the light of the gibbous moon.

> The big car flashes before them, a huge, dark flash, without lights, seemingly without sound. It comes out of the dark corn and fills the air right in front of them the way a big flat fish will glide into view suddenly in an aquarium tank. It seems to be no more than a yard in front of their headlights. Then it's gone—it has disappeared into the corn on the other side of the road. . . . What they feel is not terror or thanksgiving—not yet. What they feel is strangeness. They feel as strange, as flattened out and borne aloft, as unconnected with previous and future events as the ghost car was, the black fish. The shaggy branches of the pine trees are moving overhead, and under those branches the moonlight comes clear on the hesitant grass of their new lawn.
>
> "Are you guys dead?" Eva says, rousing them. "Aren't we home?"

The power and effectiveness of this moment in a story that has been all about the difficulty of moving forward, given how the luggage of history and expectation make arrival so difficult, is remarkable. It makes clear what it really is to be cut off from the past and the future. We could marvel at a story that seems to define through narrative the rising black, and then finds a way to give the metaphor a literal embodiment—it's an astounding accomplishment. But my interest is to suggest how you might work to create such moments in your own fiction.

Let me state the obvious: to say the encounter with the Dodge is a moment in which the characters experience a comic-book alternate universe diminishes the story. However, after you've read and considered the story, and if you wish for it to serve as a practical model, it may be useful to think of it as an encounter with an alternate universe, a universe in which "the dark things that always rise up" have a physical presence—it's where they live.

Munro is careful to make it clear that they are on a real road with real intersections, and the vehicle that passes before them is a 1969 Dodge. There is nothing mystical about drunken boys driving in the dark. The Dodge is a real vehicle, but the experience of Roberta and George is otherworldly, and Munro describes it as such. "It comes out of the dark corn and fills the air . . . the way a big flat fish will glide into view suddenly in an aquarium tank." Compare this to Marilynne Robinson: "There was a trembling. . . . The whole long bridge was as quick and tense as vertebrae. . . . Shock banged and pounded in every joint. I saw a light pass over my head like a meteor." Is there anything more otherworldly than a meteor? Something else happens in this episode from *Housekeeping:* the girl calls her aunt by a different name—the name of her dead mother. Clearly, the girl responds to the moment as if it was a glimpse into another world.

Any writer who has read much Munro has felt pangs of envy, and many have thought, "In this next draft, I'll make my story as complex as Alice Munro's stories." Yet few, it seems, have succeeded. Thinking about the alternate universe when you revise will not make your stories the equal of Munro's; however, it may wedge open the story and permit you to find something new. My advice is to go over your drafts and look for the shimmer—the bridge—moments that encourage you to show a glimpse of another world.

One more thing before moving on: you may think the Dodge obviously represents death, and that's the other world of the story. Maybe you're right and maybe not. But this is not the way to think while you're writing. If you do, you'll come up with something logical, a metaphor that fits too neatly. Instead, you need to sink into the story you've written and let it determine the crossing point.

Examine the metaphors and similes, the actions of the characters, the descriptions of place—listen to what you've already written and let it advise you.

I will suggest three more practical ways that this metaphor may be applied, with a story to illustrate each.

Alice Elliott Dark's "In the Gloaming" is told from the point of view of a woman whose son has come home to die. At the opening of the story, Laird announces he does not want to entertain any more visitors. The story follows Laird and his mother, Janet, from this point of exclusion to his death; the story is shaped around his dying, which is defined as a process of exclusion. Another narrative shape, his mother's recognition that Laird has been the love of her life, underlies the first; this romance between mother and son, like any romance, is also defined as a kind of exclusion. Both shapes are organic to the characters, products of Laird's limited stamina and his decision to eliminate contact with others in order to reserve his strength.

Janet recognizes that her son is most able to be "his *old* old self" during the twilight hours. The gloaming may seem like a heavy-handed metaphor for the "twilight of life," but Dark gets away with it because the story has a beautifully designed structure. The gloaming is the time when Laird is magically restored, and it restores his mother, as well. She becomes a girl in love, instead of a mother losing a son. The story alternates between narration and scene, but the only moments of pure scene are those that occur in the gloaming. The structure thus invisibly reinforces what the narrative is showing—that the moments in the gloaming are special.

Dark also makes the scenes grow progressively shorter as Laird's strength fades and he moves closer to death. The first scene is two and a half pages, the next is two and a quarter, then two pages, then one half page, one quarter page.

This structure permits Dark to orchestrate the ending. Laird's final experience of the gloaming is a false one; the dimness that he perceives is not caused by the end of day but by the failing of his vision. It would have been contrived to have his death occur during the gloaming, but there is no coincidence in his vision failing as death takes hold of him. This false gloaming is treated structurally as if it were genuine, which creates the impression that the story has gone as far as it can go. But the story then exceeds its promise, and in doing so exceeds the reader's expectations, creating in the process a rush of emotional power.

Because Laird experiences his final gloaming in the daylight, the real gloaming on the day of his death is yet to come. It is then that Laird's father, Martin, is able to speak with Janet. We believe that he has chosen to withdraw from them, and there's some truth to that, but we have experienced the story from Janet's point of view and so we've never questioned whether his withdrawal is tied to *her* desire to have Laird to herself, to Laird and Janet's mutual desire to exclude. We have taken at face value Janet's assumption that Martin is not paying attention, and so we feel complicit when she discovers her error.

Dark writes: "Martin came in. Janet was watching the trees turn to mere silhouettes against the darkening sky." This is how she lets us know that they are in the gloaming and conversation—real human connection—is possible. Martin suggests bagpipes for the funeral, and Janet is surprised that he is so much in tune with their son's desires. "In a breath it would be night," Dark writes, and Martin says, "Please tell me—what else did my boy like?" This line delivers an overwhelming emotional punch, and it avoids sentimentality by means of Janet's error and the reader's culpability in it.

The structure permits the final gloaming to surprise the reader and yet seem exactly right. Because the story is shaped by exclusion, Martin's knowledge of Laird also surprises and moves the reader. Our understanding of Martin changes. Our understanding of the family expands, and this is often what moves a reader—to suddenly see the larger picture.

The gloaming is the bridge, a time of day that transports the character into another dimension wherein his body is not ravaged, wherein Janet's love for her son has expression that is not tragic but joyous. The extreme and ongoing and seemingly unremitting circumstances find a daily moment of remittance, of magic.[1]

Alice Munro is known for her ability to create a sense of place, and one leaves the story "Friend of My Youth" with a rich feeling for the Ottawa Valley.

> When my mother was a young woman . . . she went to teach . . . in the Ottawa Valley. The school was on a corner of the farm that belonged to the Grieves family—a very good farm for that country. Well-drained fields with none of the Precambrian rock shouldering through the soil, a little willow-edged river running alongside, a sugar bush, log barns, and a large, unornamented house whose wooden walls had never been painted but had been left to weather. And when wood weathers in the Ottawa Valley, my mother said, I do not know why this is, but it never turns gray, it turns black. There must be something in the air she said. She often spoke of the Ottawa Valley . . . in a dogmatic, mystified way, emphasizing things about it that distinguished it from any other place on earth.

While the mother's "dogmatic, mystified" description of the Ottawa Valley is tinted with nostalgia and longing, the narrator offers a corrective:

> Of course I was disappointed when I finally got to see this place. It was not a valley at all, if by that you mean a cleft between hills; it was a mixture of flat fields and low rocks

------

1. Another story that uses this strategy, though to very different effect, is Jhumpa Lahiri's "A Temporary Matter" in her celebrated collection *Interpreter of Maladies*.

and heavy bush and little lakes—a scrambled, disarranged sort of country with no easy harmony about it, not yielding readily to any description.

The landscape is exaggerated and transformed by the narrator's mother, while the narrator's firsthand response is colored by her disappointment. The reader comes away with competing versions of the setting, which, in turn, creates yet another vision in the reader's mind, a combined vision that is not just complex but almost mythic.

QUESTION: What does the place actually look like?
ANSWER: *It depends on who you are.*

Ultimately, "Friend of My Youth" is set in *my* Ottawa Valley. And that's just the beginning. Munro uses the same bifocality to make the characters larger than life, and lend to them a sense of the mythic. There is *my* Flora Grieves, *my* Nurse Atkinson. Even the central events that take place in the story are viewed differently by mother and daughter, leaving them open for the reader's interpretation.

Take a look again at a previously quoted paragraph, slightly recast:

> It is not a story at all, if by that you mean a cleft between two characters; it is a mixture of flat dreams and low gossip and heavy history and little relief—a scrambled, disarranged sort of story with no easy harmony about it, not yielding readily to any description.

Munro's goal in her stories is often like this; she wishes to make a compelling narrative that does not resemble any of the stories with which we're familiar. Her work expands beyond any familiar definition of short story. The stories refuse to conform to current fashion or standard practice. In "Friend of My Youth," Munro takes the interesting but relatively simple étude of the Grieves family and makes of it a symphony.

The story's narrative strategy is not easy to describe. The core story is one that the narrator heard from her mother, but she does not tell it exactly as her mother did. It becomes evident that there are, in essence, two narrators, daughter and mother, and they are not entirely compatible; moreover, the narrator seems to be telling the story in order to reveal her mother or her relationship with her mother, even though neither mother nor daughter is a key character in the core story. The story's point of view, one might even argue, is also its subject; in which case, the story of the Grieves family is merely the prism through which the point of view's complexity is revealed.

"Friend of My Youth" opens with the primary narrator (the daughter) reporting a dream that features her mother, restored from debility and free of the tension that defined this daughter/ mother relationship. The narrator then recounts (and uses her own scrutiny to construct) the tale she heard from her mother about the time when she was a young teacher living on the Grieves farm. The narrator uses multiple sources to retell her mother's story, and the reader comes to understand that the narrator's mother used many sources to create her narrative, which moves back in time to a period long before she arrived in the Ottawa Valley.

Neither of our narrative sources is present in the story of Flora and Ellie Grieves and their triangle with Robert Deal. It begins with Flora engaged to farmhand Robert Deal, and adolescent Ellie acting as their mischievous companion. From this chronologically distant point, the story moves forward through Flora and Robert's courtship, Ellie's sudden aberrant behavior, the discovery of Ellie's pregnancy, her abrupt marriage to Robert Deal, the division of the house into separate halves, Ellie's string of miscarriages, and Ellie's failing physical and mental health. When the narrator's mother comes to the Ottawa Valley to teach, she resides with Flora in her half of the house for two school terms, and she becomes emotionally attached to Flora. During the second year, Nurse Atkinson arrives to care for the rapidly deteriorating Ellie.

The narrator's mother moves away from the Ottawa Valley to be married, but the story on the Grieves farm continues, leaving the narrators once again without any immediate knowledge of the events. Letters, gossip, a few facts, speculation, hearsay, romanticized ideas, imagined encounters, logic, fantasies, cynical notions, and nocturnal dreams are used to construct the remainder of the story. Ellie is dying, and the narrator's mother's friend from the post office speculates that Flora will finally get to marry Robert Deal and start a family. The narrator's mother, herself about to marry, silently agrees with this sentiment, happy that Flora will get her just reward. Instead, after Ellie dies, Robert Deal marries Nurse Atkinson, and they live on in one half of the house, painting over the black wood and having electricity installed, while Flora's side of the dwelling remains black and without lights. Eventually, Flora moves into town.

As with the setting, the narrative is evoked by a multiplicity of interpretations. For example, the Grieveses are Reformed Presbyterians, a severe sect once known as Cameronians. Early on, the narrator explains that the family's backward ways (the house unpainted and without electricity, the family without a car) is not "in the Grieveses' case a sign of poverty but of policy. . . . Some people thought this was because they were Cameronians . . . but . . . their church . . . did not forbid engines or electricity." Like the wood that weathers black, the family's backwardness seems the special detail that defines them. The narrator tells the reader that the Grieveses' religion is *not* the cause of this backwardness (despite what people believe), but no other cause is named, and so the reader will likely assume the religion *is* the source. The reader is encouraged to make assumptions. The layered point of view invites interpretation and reinterpretation. Ultimately, the narrator will even have a different interpretation of the dream that opens the story. By the story's end, virtually everything will be open to new interpretation.

For example, while reading the story, we're encouraged to see the narrator's mother and Flora as friends, and Nurse Atkinson as an interloper. In retrospect, however, we may come to a different conclusion.

Nurse Atkinson is described as "a stout woman with corsets as stiff as barrel hoops, marcelled hair the color of brass candlesticks, a mouth shaped by lipstick beyond its own stingy outlines." Whose similes are these? The narrator's, based on what her mother said? Or her mother's, as recalled faithfully by her daughter? Our view of Nurse Atkinson is based on both narrators' biased reports, many of which depend on gossip and innuendo; for instance, that Nurse Atkinson drives her own car fuels speculation about the sources of her income and the quality of her character. Because she marries Robert Deal after Ellie dies, the mother sees her as parallel to Ellie—someone who improperly takes Robert from Flora. But Munro offers the reader a parallel that neither narrator recognizes: Nurse Atkinson is a female outsider who comes to live with the Grieveses; she's parallel to the narrator's mother.

Here's an example of the parallel. The subject is Flora's mad housework:

> "I wondered if we could have a little less of the running and clattering?" said Nurse Atkinson with offensive politeness. "I only ask for my patient's sake."

It is easy for the reader to hear that "offensive politeness" and the smug tone, but how different is it from the narrator's mother calling Flora (while she's cleaning) a "whirling dervish"? This, too, is offered politely, but the narrator's mother fears that she may have offended Flora. And though Flora is not offended by "whirling dervish," the narrator's mother nonetheless assumes that Flora is indeed insulted by Nurse Atkinson's request—an assumption that the reader may be persuaded to accept.

The real accusation against Nurse Atkinson is the charge of modernity. She is a modern woman in a backward house. She smokes.

She wears makeup. She drives. She makes pudding from a package. She listens to the radio. Meanwhile, the narrator's mother, we're told, "belonged to the first generation of young women who saved their money and paid for their own weddings." In other words, she's a modern woman herself. About these two modern females, we have the following comparison: "they were around the same age—both stylish, intelligent women who liked a good time and had modern ideas. [Nurse Atkinson] offered to teach my mother to drive the car. She offered her cigarettes."

Nurse Atkinson may be guilty of occasional self-righteousness and self-congratulation, but these are the same traits that lead the narrator's mother to make assumptions about Nurse Atkinson. Munro even goes so far as to give Nurse Atkinson the story's most objective and trustworthy insight about the Grieves family. "It's not that they're poor," she says. "Or it's not even their religion. So what is it? They do not care!" Munro can get away with this overt and accurate pronouncement without diminishing the story's tension and mystery precisely because the reader is likely to dismiss anything that comes from Nurse Atkinson.

The narrator's mother sees her relationship with Flora as special, and she conveyed the story to her daughter with this slant. The daughter questions things about her mother's story, but she does not question her mother's relationship with Flora. Munro makes the teacher and the nurse equals in the household, but she filters the point of view through the teacher by way of the teacher's daughter, and so the reader is initially inclined to accept the teacher's vision of her privileged position with Flora.

Flora is not affronted—or affected—by either of them. Rather, the narrator's mother is offended on Flora's behalf, and so we are presented with an unsympathetic view of Nurse Atkinson, even though she behaves no differently than the mother.

Here, then, is the story's complex narrative strategy: the dual narrators construct and interpret the material in a complicated fashion, and Munro encourages the reader to create his own version of events from these competing visions; at the same time,

Munro permits the discerning reader to see yet another reality—one that is not entirely true to either narrator's understanding and is not likely identical to the reader's initial interpretation.

This ornate point-of-view construct permits Munro to use the reader's own biases as part of the narrative structure. The reader becomes something like a third narrator, and the reader's take on the story is no purer than that of the daughter or mother. For example, the reader is likely to feel that Flora has indeed been cheated out of her rightful marriage to Robert Deal. But the story is not kind to the institution of marriage. It is seen as something always evaluated and interpreted on faith rather than by the evidence at hand. It is this blind faith in marriage that colors the mother's vision of the story, a faith—Munro seems to suggest—that is as extreme and unlikely as a cult religion. The narrator's mother continues to see Flora as one robbed of matrimonial fulfillment, even though her own marriage becomes "a prison." Upon hearing the story as an adolescent, the narrator longs for Robert Deal even though she's told what marriage does to Ellie.

The parallel between religious faith and this faith in marriage is explored in interesting ways, especially concerning the idea of martyrdom. If the narrator's mother had written down her version of the core story (*The Maiden Lady*), Flora would have been presented as a martyr, one who goes on bravely in the face of betrayal, who forgives the unfaithful without complaint, who is a saint because she has been robbed of her rightful matrimony and yet uncomplainingly serves those who betrayed her. Yet within Munro's story, martyrdom seems tied to *getting* married, not to missing out on it. Both Ellie and the narrator's mother make sacrifices and suffer greatly to advance a cause. Their cause is marriage, and they are martyrs to it.

Near the end of "Friend of My Youth," after the core story has been fully elaborated, the narrator imagines Flora living in town, working in a retail store. "I would have wanted to tell her that I knew . . . her story, though we had never met." She understands while recalling the fantasy that it is something like a dream:

[Flora] is not surprised that I am telling her this, but she is weary of it, of me and my idea of her . . . my notion that I can know anything about her.

Of course it's my mother I'm thinking of . . . as she was in those dreams. . . . But I now recall that I was disconcerted as well. I felt slightly cheated. . . . Offended, tricked, cheated, by this welcome turnaround, this reprieve. My mother moving rather carelessly out of her old prison, showing options and powers I never dreamed she had, changes more than herself. She changes the bitter lump of love I have carried all this time into a phantom—something useless and uncalled for, like a phantom pregnancy.

Flora and her mother merge in dreamlike fashion. The narrator, who sees that neither she nor her mother ever could understand Flora, recognizes that this must also apply to her own understanding of her mother. And it is for this that she wishes forgiveness, for having assumed to know so much about her mother that she could feel self-righteous and self-congratulatory. The differing takes on the story of Flora Grieves become a metaphor for the estrangement between mother and daughter. And the narrator understands that the easy forgiveness she loved in those dreams is a betrayal; it would change the actual love she possesses for her mother, turning it into "something . . . like a phantom pregnancy." It was, of course, Ellie who had the phantom pregnancies, and by using this simile, Munro links the multiple stories together in an intricate imagistic web.

The story would seem to be over, but Munro is not finished. After a space break comes the final paragraph, which ends as follows:

The Cameronians—for a long time they have preferred to be called the Reformed Presbyterians—went into battle singing the seventy-fourth and the seventy-eighth Psalms. They hacked the haughty Bishop of St. Andrews to death

on the highway and rode their horses over his body. One
of their ministers, in a mood of firm rejoicing at his own
hanging, excommunicated all the other preachers in the
world.

This story about point of view and interpretation, about
marriage and religion and martyrdom, ends with a minister ex-
communicating all others upon his imminent martyrdom, denying that anyone but he can interpret the Bible and the story of its
martyr. The Cameronians, we are reminded, are simply a type of
Presbyterian, and so the story's final turn celebrates and indicts
all Christians (not just the fringe elements) for believing in a story
that is contradicted by virtually every scrap of knowledge that
humankind has accumulated, a story that must be taken utterly
on faith. The Cameronians are separated in their beliefs from the
great body of Christians worldwide because they have a slightly
different interpretation of that old, unlikely tale.

This final movement is pure Munro. Having completed the
narrative of the characters, it steps outside the normal bounds of
story to suggest that the personal narratives of the characters embody in their actions something essential to the understanding of
humankind.

You may be asking what any of this has to do with the idea of an
alternate universe. Consider the quotation that follows:

> The odd thing is that my mother's ideas were in line with
> some progressive notions of her times, and mine echoed
> the notions that were favored in my time. . . . It's as if ten-
> dencies that seem most deeply rooted in our minds, most
> private and singular, have come in as spores on the prevail-
> ing wind.

The narrator and her mother, though living in isolated places,
are still members of the culture, and they are influenced by it. But

Flora Grieves is *not*. She is not opposed to modernity; she simply doesn't care about it. She is not opposed to electricity; she simply doesn't care about it. Everyone who attempts to describe what happens in the Grieveses' household ascribes to Flora her own desires, her own grievances, her own articles of faith. Flora is affected by none of them. *Flora is not of this world.*

How could any one of us ever write a story of such beauty and complexity?

I honestly don't know. This is one of the best stories I've ever read, and I have no idea how to emulate it. However, you may want to think about what it is like to have among you a person who is from another universe, and yet everyone around her is certain they know her. What they decide, of course, reveals them, not the alien, who remains unknowable.

The final strategy involves travel—a character going off on a trip that takes him to an alternate universe. Ernest Hemingway's story "Indian Camp" is wonderful to study for a number of reasons—the elegant shape of journey and return, the powerful encounters with life and death, and Hemingway's great gift for leaving the most important things unsaid. The story opens as follows:

> At the lake shore there was another rowboat drawn up. The two Indians stood waiting.
>
> Nick and his father got in the stern of the boat and the Indians shoved it off and one of them got in to row. Uncle George sat in the stern of the camp rowboat. . . .
>
> The two boats started off in the dark.

A few lines later:

> Uncle George was smoking a cigar in the dark. The young Indian pulled the boat way up on the beach. Uncle George gave both the Indians cigars.

They walked up from the beach through a meadow that was soaking wet with dew.

You may be running ahead of me, thinking that this is a story of a journey by boat to an alternate universe. The journey has a specific function for Nick's father, a doctor, and while he performs his obvious task well—a cesarean delivery—he does not understand all of the terms of the foreign world; as a result, the acts that seem initially heroic have tragic results when the woman's injured husband kills himself. The great white doctor fails even as he succeeds.

This is a legitimate reading, but it's just a portion of what's going on. The key to a larger understanding of the story is that the main character is a child. His father does indeed take him into an alternate universe, but it is the universe of adults. We are the aliens in this story, a whole world of people that, as far as Nick is concerned, might as well all be Flora Grieves.

The story shows the boy what the adult universe has to offer—the suffering required to bring about life, and the fact and finality of death. But Nick, though he witnesses much, is unable to understand this world. The final line makes this very clear: "He felt quite sure that he would never die." This is the thought of a child. He has made the journey into the alternate universe, witnessed the actions of adults, and returns largely unchanged.

What is crucial, then, is all that Nick witnesses but does *not* understand, everything that makes up the secret language of that alternate universe. Nick sees his uncle George handing out cigars, but he does not know that in the adult world this is what fathers do when their children are born. He hears the woman cry out when George enters the room while her husband lies in the top bunk. He witnesses the woman choosing George's arm to bite as she suffers through labor. He sees the conspiratorial look of the younger Indian with George. He sees, too, that the husband, who has already cut himself once, now cuts his own throat. He knows that George fetched his father and is aware that George stays behind. But these gestures and actions are part of a language that is foreign to him. He cannot *read* them. He does not see how they can ever apply to him.

> "Why did he kill himself, Daddy?"
> "I don't know, Nick. He couldn't stand things, I guess."
> "Do many men kill themselves, Daddy?"
> "Not very many, Nick."
> "Do many women?"
> "Hardly ever."
> "Don't they ever?"
> "Oh, yes. They do sometimes."
> "Daddy?"
> "Yes."
> "Where did Uncle George go?"

It is important to read fiction on its own terms. Writers need to read as people who are passionate about literature and the world, and in love with narrative. At some point, however, it can be useful to have specific pragmatic strategies for thinking about stories. And this strategy of the alternate universe may provide a means to revise and rethink those stories that adamantly refuse to become magical, stories wherein you have successfully created that great dark fish, but you cannot make it surface.

This essay refers to the following creative works:
    Billy Budd, Sailor by Herman Melville
    Pigs in Heaven by Barbara Kingsolver
    Before and After by Rosellen Brown
    American Owned Love by Robert Boswell

POLITICS AND ART IN THE NOVEL

My family and I spend the summers in Colorado, high in the Rockies, in the ski town of Telluride. We stay in a miner's shack that is one hundred years old. Repairs often fall to my uncalloused hands. The most demanding task one summer was the dismantling of an old garage bermed into the mountainside. The walls of the garage were made of stacked rock, railroad ties, and scrap lumber. The roof of the garage consisted of thirty-five telephone poles. My job was to cut up all the poles and ties, and haul it all away. Picture a man standing on the roof of a garage with a chain saw and sledgehammer, cutting away at the telephone poles at his feet. I knew I had a conflict, but I wasn't sure whether it was man versus nature, man versus man, man versus himself—or (d) all of the above.

The telephone poles had been treated with creosote, which meant that my clothes got coated with a sticky film, as did my face and hands. Sawdust adhered to the creosote like an extra layer of skin. I looked like I'd been tarred and woodchipped.

One day while I was standing on the muddy garage floor, sawing the big pieces into smaller ones, the idling chain saw growling in my hand, a neighbor from across the street, a smartly dressed woman in her forties, approached me and said, "Could you possibly quit that? I'm a writer and I can't work with that noise."

I smiled widely, sawdust exaggerating the lines in my face as if I were a cartoon drawing, chain saw sputtering loudly in my gloved hand, and said, "I'm a writer, too!"

Never in my life have I felt more like the Disney character Goofy.

My neighbor glanced around nervously and said, "I *see*."

Not one who gives up easily (or learns quickly), I said, "Do you write fiction or nonfiction?"

"Nonfiction," she told me, backing away cautiously.

The conversation deteriorated from there. I agreed to quit chainsawing for the day so she could write. I've often felt like an impostor, but never more so than on this occasion. It annoyed me that I felt that way, as if I believed a writer was someone who shouldn't get his hands dirty. I was working at the time on a novel with political undertones, and it occurred to me that I might cut an equally ridiculous figure as an author as I did in that failing garage. Which led me to think about what it meant to be a writer and—oh, you get the picture: I started, once again, to question how I was spending my life.

Like many writers, my life has been directed by multiple forces. One powerful force has always been literature and writing, but another has been the desire to usher along justice. My adolescence took place in the sixties and seventies . . . and, well, the eighties and nineties and is still running strong in the new century, but it *began* in the sixties, a convenient time for the incipient writer to begin refiguring the world aesthetically and politically, as it was a time of powerful disillusionment with the status quo. Many of the sources of disillusionment were concrete, most notably the war in Vietnam and the resistance encountered by the civil rights movement. My father had been the principal of the elementary school I attended in Wickliffe, Kentucky, a segregated school until he worked to integrate it (on his own) when I was in the fourth grade. I didn't have to be particularly sensitive or empathetic to be aware of racial injustice—it was thrust in my face. Similarly, the war in Vietnam was no abstract issue. My final year of high school I used to lie awake at night making a series of plans for what to do if I got a low lottery number in the draft. In my noblest of moods, I pictured myself going to prison rather than joining the fray, shackled but unswayed, my head held high. More often and more realistically, I imagined becoming a fry cook in Vancouver. Everyone knew somebody who was in Vietnam or back from it or who had failed to come back. Not abstract in the least, the war was all too real.

And people did something about it. They marched and protested; they wrote political poetry and political novels. While it would be wrong to say they prevailed, they did make a difference. Popular opinion changed so dramatically that even Nixon ran as a peace candidate, and the dread and suspicion left over from the Vietnam experience made it difficult—for a long while, anyway— for people in power to play at war.

That time, however, was long ago, and the powers of stasis have since convinced us that change is no longer possible, that we are powerless to influence world events or national politics. Have you had a conversation like this? It starts with some mention of an unjust act or a bit of political disgrace, then it moves more specifically to some immediate travesty taking place in D.C.; much ranting follows about evil men in elected positions, and then one participant throws up his hands and says, "What are we to do?" or, "There's no point in making ourselves upset about it," or, "I feel so helpless."

This conversation recurred in my living room with a good friend, a professor in the humanities, and when the conversation took that final turn, she said, "I feel so helpless to do anything about it." I almost responded in kind, but it struck me that we were both university professors and well published in our fields, and that my automatic agreement would be a lie. I was a writer and she, a history professor. How could we pretend to be helpless? I said as much, and she agreed to a certain extent, but added that it seemed impossible to make a difference, that we could write and teach and fight the good fight, but we were going to lose, and it was obvious we were going to lose. Nothing was going to change.

I began thinking about "learned helplessness," that old term from Psych 101. Two groups of monkeys in cages with electrified floors were treated to shocks on a regular basis. One group found it could escape the shocks by leaping onto a little shelf; the other group learned there was no way to escape the shocks. Later, when the second group was given a shelf on which to escape, they could not learn to jump up on it to avoid the shocks. They had already learned that they were helpless.

We seem to have "learned" that it is impossible to effect a change, and we believe it, even though in our lifetime we have witnessed the sudden death of Stalinism in Central Europe and the demise of the Soviet Union—political changes of enormous magnitude. In the United States, we have seen the civil rights movement make it much more difficult for public institutions to maintain their long-held hierarchies; this is not to say that we live free of prejudice, but that we have made progress in eliminating the institutional constructs of prejudice, and that is no small matter.

I could go on, but my point is simple: change is possible.

Yet when writers attempt to engage political issues in their narratives, they find the task extraordinarily difficult—if the objective is also to create a literary story. Many of the most effective political novels have had little literary ambition. Harriet Beecher Stowe's *Uncle Tom's Cabin* had a powerful effect on the nation's attitudes toward slavery, and anyone with any sense is grateful for its publication. However, it is a dreadful novel by virtually every literary measure. The characters are one-dimensional, the episodes are melodramatic, and the political argument has the subtlety of a sledgehammer. Politically speaking, *Uncle Tom's Cabin* is a very important novel. As a work of art, it has no importance whatsoever. *None.*

One would think that these two types of measurement could

be kept distinct, but it is not a simple matter; moreover, it is not the topic I'm addressing in this essay. I have no idea how to advise anyone about the writing of a political novel that has no interest in being a work of art. Even the most basic of tenets—be honest, make your characters fully rounded—may be a handicap if you're concerned with nothing but influencing the reader's politics. I address this essay, then, to writers who want to write good books and who do not wish to ignore or deny the circumstances of the world around them.

The literary writer knows—perhaps all too well—that political fervor at the expense of one's craft or the book's honesty will result in propaganda, a too-easy argument that will have little or no effect on any knowledgeable reader. Workshops tend to aggressively discourage political writing. For most apprentice writers (for that matter, the rest of us, too), the task of creating a full and meaningful narrative is, by itself, daunting. The added responsibilities that arise when stories have overt political aims get ignored or are badly handled. The larger problems with the story may be difficult to name, but the interference of the political message is usually painfully obvious, and so the workshop criticism will home in on it. Everyone else in the workshop is thereby discouraged from including politics in future stories. Yet, while dealing with politics in fiction is a higher-order problem, that doesn't mean that you shouldn't try it.

It's fair to ask, just what are those "added responsibilities"? I'll address that question with the help of an essay by Noam Chomsky on the political responsibilities of the intellectual. I think the responsibilities of the political novelist are largely the same. Chomsky did not make a list, but I culled three essentials from his essay.

1. *It is the responsibility of intellectuals to speak the truth and to expose lies.*
This statement may appear straightforward, but its application is complicated. It means that if you're writing a novel that engages a specific political issue, your obligation is to embody the best

argument for *both* sides of the issue, regardless of your personal stand on the matter. Otherwise, you're lying.

In a novel, you create a world and if you create a world that conveniently reinforces your political beliefs, you're lying—even if you're basing the book on real events. Because you have such incredible creative license, you cannot make a viable political statement if you do not acknowledge the full range of possibilities that reside within the issue as it pertains to your characters. This may lead you to the uncomfortable situation of discovering or inventing strong arguments for positions you do *not* hold.

Personally, I think the gun laws in our country are inadequate. I don't think it's reasonable to accept that a certain number of children will be gunned down in classrooms each year, or that parts of every American city are like war zones. I don't claim to have the answer to the problem, but I believe we need to take steps. However, in writing fiction about guns and gun ownership, I stumbled upon an argument for keeping weapons that, for me, is more convincing than any of the NRA's contentions: owning a gun may make you *feel* less helpless. It's entirely possible that my own belief in engaging the political world through writing fiction amounts to the same kind of intellectual dodge and emotional crutch. I certainly hope it's something more than that, but I know that part of the reason I write is to fight that sense of helplessness we've all learned so well.

2. When we consider the responsibility of intellectuals, our basic concerns must be their role in the creation and analysis of ideology.

Any political novel that merely reiterates or embodies an existing ideology is not a work of art, because a knowledgeable reader (in this case, one familiar with the ideology) will not be asked to alter her vision. Such a novel is merely the handmaiden of the ideology, a servant to theory, and this servitude usually comes at the expense of believable characters and a viable story. If what the literary novel is asked to do is poke through the illusions a culture clings to, thereby altering how the reader sees the culture, then a novel that merely illustrates an ideology takes as truth that ideology. This would function as the framework for a novel only if that ideology were wholly comprehensive and foolproof. A fundamentalist Christian may well think of the church's teachings in this manner—comprehensive and foolproof—and there are plenty of tales of the advantages of the Christian life that masquerade as novels. Of course, there are also plenty of religious literary writers, but you aren't going to find Flannery O'Connor or Walker Percy taught in Bible school. They push at the limits of the accepted interpretations and suggest ironies that the church may wish to ignore. It's one thing to say that God is watching us all, and quite another to suggest by means of an execution that there's a divine gun to your head every minute of your life. Their fictions analyze the accepted teachings; they create new modes of thought.

Very often, for a writer, ideology is the light that creates the darkness. While we are all obliged to study ideologies and permit them to inform the way we comprehend the world, when we go to write we must be careful not to let them overtly guide us. Like a flashlight on a dark night, ideology will brightly illuminate patches of the landscape, but it makes all that is not lit that much harder to see. It's better for the writer to turn off the light and let her eyes adjust to the dark. Of course, I do not mean to suggest that writers must be immune to the gigantic philosophical works of the past centuries, but they must not merely adopt an ideological stance and let it dictate their fiction.

3. *If it is the responsibility of the intellectual to insist upon the truth, it is also his duty to see events in their historical perspective.*
Earlier in this book, I referred to Herman Melville's novella *Billy Budd, Sailor* as an example of the first-person omniscient narrator. It is also, I believe, a remarkable work of political fiction. In the late 1980s, I gave a class on *Billy Budd* and argued that if you wanted to understand what was going on in the Soviet Union, you

were better off reading Melville than listening to Peter Jennings. Mikhail Gorbachev, at that time, was fighting Lithuania's attempt to exit the Soviet Union, while also suggesting that slower, legal means were available to accomplish that goal. He sent troops to quell the uprising, and innocents were slaughtered. I encouraged students to look at Gorbachev as one might look at Vere. I suggested that his sending of troops might be understood as an act he felt necessary to avoid a "mutiny"—a takeover by hard-liners, the old-time Stalinists.[1]

The newsmen who had glorified Gorbachev had turned on him ruthlessly when the Lithuanian fighting began, and neither the glorification nor the vilification captured the situation. The power of great political fiction is that it continues telling the truth and providing historical perspective—even for events that may take place one hundred years after the story's inception.

Of course, political novels may work by different means to provide historical perspective. Take, for example, Don DeLillo's *White Noise*, a novel that uses exaggeration and satire to make the reader recognize the political terms of her own life. DeLillo's main character is chair of Hitler Studies at a small college, and one of his academic colleagues exclusively studies car-crash sequences. Extrapolate the distance between current academic fashion and DeLillo's scenario, and you have the satiric distance by which to negotiate the remainder of the novel—and the historical perspective the novel requires.

------

1. Some months after my lecture on *Billy Budd*, the mutiny that Starry Gorbachev feared did, indeed, take place, although it was only temporarily successful. The lecture was based on my interpretations of Melville's novella and a sociological paper written by my brother, Terry Boswell, about the likelihood of revolution in the Soviet Union and elsewhere in light of Nikolai Kondratiev's long wave theory. The paper, written in 1986, suggested the likelihood of revolutions toppling the Soviet Union, and it might have made my brother one of the better-known sociologists in the country, but the journal took more than two years to print it, and it came out just after the demise of the Soviet Union. Terry Boswell died in June 2006 from complications related to ALS.

Given Chomsky's three basic responsibilities (combined with the demands of literary fiction), I offer the following simple strategies for the literary writer who wishes to engage politics in her fiction.

Strategy One: Write from the point of view of the other.
When I lived in Arizona, I had a passing involvement with the Sanctuary Movement, the underground railroad designed to protect Central Americans who had come to the United States seeking asylum. Because the U.S. supported the governments they had fled and refused to acknowledge that such governments tortured and killed dissidents, these refugees were rarely offered legal sanctuary by our government. If caught, they were routinely sent back, which often meant imprisonment, torture, or execution. I believed then, and still believe, that the moral and ethical thing to do was to break the law and help hide these political refugees. I include this because it's important that you know my biases.

I attended a benefit play written by members of the Sanctuary Movement. I was, to say the least, predisposed to like the performance. It was the story of two people fleeing Guatemala after the execution of family members, their arrival in the U.S. after an arduous journey and an awful ordeal with a coyote (who almost suffocates them in a van, smuggling them across the border), the raw deal they get, and their impending return to Guatemala and certain death—all orchestrated by the U.S. government. The play did not stray from historical realities and it very clearly reflected my political beliefs, and I've never hated any performance half as much.

The main characters were so noble they seemed to deserve martyrdom. They were utterly flawless, while the opposition—government forces mainly—were all monsters in reflecting sunglasses, the kind of people at whom, in movies, dogs will instinctively snarl. The heroes were victims and the political message was hammered at with a ruthlessness that would make the most abusive coyote look like Gandhi.

We were supposed to pity the refugees, but all I felt was anger. A true and powerful story had been turned into a bit of self-serving, hackneyed, humorless, boring, clichéd propaganda. Part of the problem was simply bad writing, but a greater part of it stemmed from the decision to make the main characters victims. One of the common properties of victimization is the stripping away of one's identity: a person being beaten bleeds, and we all bleed in more or less the same way. Without a unique and identifiable human at their center, most narratives fail. The victim almost inevitably becomes a stereotype or simply a stick figure acting out as ordered, which is to say, a victim of the *author*. Moreover, the victim (by definition an innocent) is often transformed by the narrative into a figure of self-righteousness, one who is not only morally pure, but who can show others (including, most obviously, the reader or audience member) the straight and true path.

Let me quote Philip Roth on the same subject:

> The late Polish writer Tadeusz Borowski said that the only way to write about the Holocaust was as the guilty, as the complicit and implicated: that is what he did in his first-person fictional memoir, *This Way for the Gas, Ladies and Gentlemen*. There Borowski may even have pretended to a dramatically more chilling degree of moral numbness than he felt as an Auschwitz prisoner, precisely to reveal the Auschwitz horror as the wholly innocent victims could not. I think . . . some of the most original Eastern European writers . . . have positioned themselves similarly . . . to tell us that there are no uncontaminated angels, that the evil is inside as well as outside.

The following, then, is strategy one: in situations where you see a clear injustice, situating the story in the point of view of the aggressor will more likely permit you to find the full human dimensions of both the victim and the aggressors, which, in turn, will give you the opportunity to avoid moralizing melodrama and achieve a work of literature that is also a political statement.

To make this argument clearer, let's look at a lab re-creation of Auschwitz. In the early 1960s, Yale researcher Stanley Milgram designed a famous study of what he called "destructive obedience to authority" to determine what kind of person would follow orders if those orders meant seriously damaging or even killing another person. Volunteers for his experiment were brought in to meet a man in a white lab coat who told them that the experiment had to do with learning and reinforcement. Volunteer number one would ask questions, and volunteer number two would answer them. If number two answered incorrectly, number one had to administer a shock, whose voltage increased with each missed answer. Number two was strapped into a little closet, invisible to the others. The trick was that number two was a stooge and there were no actual shocks, but the real volunteers didn't know that. They thought they were administering shocks for wrong answers, turning up the power after each miss. What they heard before long was number two screaming in pain and asking to be released, then refusing to answer (resulting in more shocks), and finally just dead silence, as if number two had passed out or died. Whenever volunteers said something like "Shouldn't we stop?" or "I don't think we should go on," the man in the white coat would say it was all fine and to continue. A startling percentage of people administered shocks beyond the point when the screaming ceased, relying on the calm authority of the man in the lab coat instead of their own moral conscience.

It was an amazing and deplorable experiment whose replication is no longer feasible; the participants experienced incredible self-recrimination afterward, and contemporary safeguards for human experimentation would not permit such a study. But my point is this: if number two had not been a stooge, just another volunteer who wound up being shocked senseless, he is the one the tabloids would rush to interview; but who would have the more interesting story? The person who just kept getting shocks no matter what he did? Or the person who slowly discovered that she was causing someone else real pain and yet did not quit because she was told by an authority figure to continue?

Writing from this point of view usually entails seducing the reader into siding with a protagonist's early actions so that when the character begins to understand his role the reader will feel culpable. By doing this, the reader cannot stand above and condemn a character's actions; rather, the reader's compassion for both the victim and the aggressor are enlarged. The story becomes more complex without hedging or apologizing for the evil of the actions.

Imagine that the Sanctuary play is remade with the main character an INS officer or simply a man who discovers his neighbors are sheltering a family of fugitives and turns them over to authorities, only to discover that the family deported because of his actions has been executed. This man's story could be quite powerful.

Strategy Two: The Contradictory Action

This is a variation of strategy one, and again it hinges on the point-of-view selection. Rather than select as your protagonist the aggressor, you select someone who shares your political beliefs but who is forced by circumstances to act in a manner contradictory to those beliefs.

In Rosellen Brown's *Before and After*, a mother and father are faced with the stunning knowledge that their son has murdered his girlfriend in a moment of rage. The father finds himself hiding evidence and breaking the law to protect his son. The father is not a criminal by nature, but the larger issue of his son's life overwhelms everything else.

This strategy encourages multifaceted characters because it demands that the protagonist perform acts that he finds loathsome. Because the reader sees the world through the character's eyes, the reader will likely find sympathy for the acts, regardless of her own political leanings. Brown's novel asks what it would take for a law-abiding citizen to break the law; another writer might ask what it would take for a practicing Catholic to support abortion, or for a pacifist to demand the death penalty. The strategy begins with a simple question: what would it take for you to act contrary to your beliefs?

Rosellen Brown takes this strategy an extra step in *Before and After*. The mother of the boy who murdered his girlfriend discovers that she will not lie to protect her son. She is a doctor and saw the bloodied corpse. She had the opportunity to imagine the type of savage that would commit such an act before discovering that it was her son who did it. Although she would have sworn to her willingness to give up her life for her son, she discovers she will not protect him. Brown provides competing responses to the murder, and the reader is likely to feel that both make sense, that both are somehow *right*.

Strategy Three: Place culturally accepted lies in opposition to each other.
The O.J. Simpson debacle was a political saga that captured the imagination of the public in an impressive and perhaps unprecedented manner, to the extent that a dozen years after the trial the very idea of a book contract going to O.J. caused enough outrage that the editor lost her job.

The O.J. story has all the elements of a good political novel, except for one thing: a conscientious author. The basic story is potentially wonderful because there are so many avenues to explore. A successful and famous black man, a former athlete of nearly mythic talent who has become a media staple with a likable persona, is accused of murdering his young, beautiful, white ex-wife and her friend. This is potent material for a political novel because it forces us to examine stereotypes that make us uncomfortable, stereotypes about black men and white women, about athletes, about blonde beauties—and we're only scratching the surface. It turns out that the black man has a history of beating the murdered woman, and there is what seems like overwhelming evidence suggesting his guilt; yet he claims he's innocent, despite some well-publicized behavior that encourages the opposite conclusion.

His defense is that the police set him up. This sounds ludicrous. True, the Los Angeles Police Department is not known for its enlightened treatment of blacks, and among several conspicuous examples of racist behavior, the Rodney King incident is both the most glaring and the most recent. But O.J. is not Rodney King. O.J. is a millionaire, a hero since his days at USC, one of the first black athletes to be idolized by all races.

Then comes evidence suggesting that the detective who supplied some of the most damning evidence has a history of incredible racism, that he and another detective have lied on the stand, that he has bragged about setting up black men, that he has a history of pulling over cars when he sees mixed-race couples and inventing charges. It is persuasively suggested that he might particularly enjoy punishing a millionaire black man with a beautiful blonde ex-wife. And it does seem that evidence has been, at the very least, mishandled. When the detective is asked under oath if he planted or tainted evidence in the case, he pleads the Fifth Amendment.

But wait, the prosecution says, despite the mess-ups and the unfortunate detective, the evidence to convict is still most impressive; moreover, don't we all really *know* that the guy did it? Are we just going to let him walk?

The jury finds him not guilty. Groups of blacks around the country cheer. Whites suggest the decision by a largely black jury was "emotional," not rational. Some pundits remind us that "not guilty" is not the same as "innocent."

I had no interest in the O.J. saga when it started. Like most of white America, I assumed he was guilty. Like the police, I reasoned that it was unlikely the victims had been killed in some random fashion. I recall talking with friends about the violent training that is a part of football and the misogyny that sometimes seems to go with it. Not that there wasn't also an element of disbelief when any of us first heard of it. There was something we had to get past in order to believe O.J. guilty. Most of us accomplished that maneuver early on, and then we forgot about it, but there was, at first, some resistance to believing it at all.

I didn't watch the chase on TV and I didn't care about the trial as long as it seemed to be merely another bit of celebrity hoopla, a stupid act of violence exploited by the media because the accused is some kind of "star." The introduction of a racist detective changed all of that. I was immediately interested in "the Fuhrman tapes"—the thirteen hours of recorded interviews between Detective Mark Fuhrman and the writer Laura McKinny. In the years since the trial, Fuhrman has done a lot to rehabilitate his image, but the power of his own words should not be forgotten. Some excerpts follow:

> You know these people here, we got all this money going to Ethiopia for what? To feed a bunch of dumb niggers that their own government won't even feed. . . .
>
> People there don't want niggers in their town. People there don't want Mexicans in their town. They don't want anybody but good people in their town, and anything you can do to get them out of there, that's fine with them. We have no niggers where I grew up.
>
> Nigger drivin' a Porsche that doesn't look like he's got a $300 suit on, you always stop him.
>
> Most real good policemen understand that they would love to take certain people to the alley and just blow their brains out.

Detective Fuhrman, it should be remembered, was the officer who found both of the incriminating gloves and some of the bloody trail. He entered Simpson's estate without a search warrant, claiming the circumstances demanded it. He lied under oath—and was later convicted of perjury.

I'd like to revisit the O.J. story as if it were a political novel.

Let's begin by considering the novel in two unsuccessful versions. First, let's imagine that the novel is written by a person whose political agenda is to the far right.

The right-wing author will emphasize certain aspects of the story at the expense of others. The police, in all likelihood, will be cast as diligent, resourceful, and honest men and women who have gotten a bad rap because of a couple of bad apples. Little did they know that one of the men on this very case would be overzealous. The fact that the accused black man is rich will not particularly be an issue, nor will the fact that he was an athlete, but how he spent his money and rumors about his loose and disreputable behavior will get plenty of play. The fact that his marriage was interracial will be subtly criticized throughout. The black man's beating of the white woman will be highlighted, a way to give lip service to women's issues while covertly hammering at the race issue. Ultimately, the noble cops and prosecutors will be undone by a judicial system that cares more about the rights of criminals than it does about the suffering of victims, and a guilty murderer will be returned to the streets.

Now let's switch over and imagine that the writer is one who succumbs to his left-wing politics. The novel will focus on the racist history of the LAPD and particularly the doings of the racist detective. The hero will be the attorney representing the defense. The fact that a rise in right-wing terrorism has resulted in the recent murders of abortion doctors, the bombing of a public building in Oklahoma City, and the fatal derailing of a train in Arizona will feature prominently in the studies of the honest lawyer trying to keep yet another black man from being railroaded into prison. The fact that the accused pulled himself up out of soul-killing poverty to succeed against great odds will be given many pages. The enormous resources that the prosecution pours into the case will be emphasized, along with their desire not to be embarrassed as they have been by recent well-publicized cases. Pressures from superiors force decent cops and prosecutors first to ignore and then to work to cover up the ugly actions of a racist detective, all of them operating under the premise of guilt rather than the presumption of innocence. One of the prosecutors will ultimately, and unethically, baldly state in court that she *knows* in her heart he did it. The tampering with the evidence will pepper the narrative like little explosions, while the history of wife beating ("spousal abuse," it'll be called in this book) is in reality a single unfortunate incident that stemmed from a racist comment that stung so deeply the otherwise decent man took it out on the person he loved most, and he wound up paying for that by losing her. He didn't blame her for leaving, but he lived with a heavy heart. The fact that she played around on the accused will be known to the reader, but the accused will not permit it to be used, wanting not to sully his wife's reputation or to damage his children's memory of their mother. Ultimately, justice prevails, and the innocent man goes home to finally see his small children again, while the attorney returns to his office, believing that the system can be made to work.

What would the literary novelist do with this story? She would want to select from the plot the story that would most powerfully and effectively speak the truth and expose lies. What truth? What lies? The truth and lies bound up in racial and gender stereotypes, in the stereotypes associated with athletes, with the legal system. These stereotypes make up systems of held beliefs, loose ideological networks that most of us buy into either as gospel or—more likely—as a kind of shorthand. We don't have the time to analyze every issue in our day-to-day lives, so we accept certain generalities that are consistent with our overall political vision. This is something like coming to an obscure office on a ballot and voting by party allegiance, figuring the odds are with you. As a novelist, your job is to analyze the things that each side takes for granted, the unexamined beliefs that I'm calling stereotypes, but that may be too strong a word. You analyze all that is usually overlooked or considered a given.

And you work to put it all in a historical perspective. If you watched any of the televised commentary, historical perspective was conspicuously absent. No one I heard commented on the racial split in reactions to the verdict in any kind of intellectual fashion, or with any sense of history. The fact is that black people in this country have a lot more reason to believe in police conspiracies than white people do. For whites, the idea of a real police conspiracy against O.J. creates a sense of disbelief that is too great to get past, far greater than the initial disbelief when they first heard that the celebrity was accused of the crime. For blacks, the idea of a police conspiracy may well be the first thing that comes to mind. In the South that I grew up in, black people accused of anything by white people were always found guilty. Many were lynched. As many as five thousand people were lynched in the United States from the period following the Civil War up to the assassination of Martin Luther King in 1968. The great majority of the lynched were black men or boys.

I don't think I need to go back over the story elements in any detail to suggest how the literary political novel would examine the story. It would work to balance the evidence as completely as possible, and then, despite the verdict, leave the actual facts of the murder impossible to decipher; which is to say, the novel would not be about who killed the blonde and her friend. The novel would be about bringing the readers into direct contact with the premises they take for granted, the premises concerning their continuing biases, their trust and distrust of the law, and so on.

You may be wondering the following: is this really a political novel? It examines political issues, but it doesn't press the reader to share the author's vision. What good is it to write a political novel about an issue if you can't convince the reader to see the world as you see it?

The key is to engage the material in such a fashion as to shift your own views. It does not mean that you flip-flop on an issue, but that your understanding of it and of your own premises become more complicated. Then, by embodying the best arguments of both sides, you have to have faith that what is going to stick with the reader is a larger understanding of the truth—and that your beliefs will claim some portion of that truth.

Strategy Four: Explore a moral dilemma.

I referred earlier to *Billy Budd, Sailor,* and this is precisely the strategy of that novella. Captain Vere is faced with the moral dilemma of releasing a man who has struck and killed a superior officer (thereby risking mutiny), or carrying through with the letter of the law and executing a man who is innocent in every sense but the technical.

Dilemma is a word often misused. Having to make a difficult decision does not necessarily constitute a dilemma. A dilemma requires that one *must* make a decision and that any of the choices has a clearly negative outcome. In *Sophie's Choice* by William Styron, a woman is told by the Gestapo to choose which of her two children will be killed. This is a legitimate dilemma.

Pigs in Heaven by Barbara Kingsolver is the rare example of a book that has received great acclaim—winning, among other things, the Los Angeles Times Book Prize for fiction—and also hit the best-seller list for a good long time. Sentence by sentence, Kingsolver writes beautifully, and she has a premise with a genuine dilemma. Here's the story: A white woman has rescued a Native American child from an abusive situation—basically, the baby is just handed over to her by a battered woman. The white woman comes to love this child as her own, finagling the paperwork to make the adoption appear legal. However, after a few years, the tribe gets wind of this illegal adoption and investigates. The essential premise, then, is that a woman who loves her child is pitted against a tribe working to stop the removal of their children and the separation of tribal members from their culture. The survival of a family is pitted against the survival of a people.

This premise is a dilemma, and it is a serious matter. In the actual world (and in Kingsolver's own Arizona), a Native American child reared by white parents was in fact taken away from those parents and brought to a reservation to live with the tribe. Many people were understandably outraged by this act, but most had no historical perspective by which to judge the situation. As we discover in *Pigs in Heaven*, there is a long and ugly history of Native American dislocation, with children often taken from their natural parents and their people. Having won legislation to stop this, the tribal nations understandably wish to make certain the laws are enforced. Balancing this on the other side of the scale: a child has been taken from the only parents she has ever known. The personal and the historical cross blades.

The novel makes it clear that the white woman loves her child, and it also provides the details and statistics that show the legitimacy of the tribe's claim. It sets in motion a narrative that leads a tribe elder to comically reinvent wise King Solomon as part of tribal lore, offering the sage advice of sawing the child in two. The premise, in its schematic design, is precisely the kind of thing I'm advocating for political novels. Yet I believe *Pigs in Heaven* is a failed effort. Despite its powerful premise and despite the author's obvious compassion and skill with language, the novel falls apart. The reasons for this failing are instructive.

The novel provides a historical context for the story, but it fails to tell the truth and expose lies, and it fails to create or analyze ideology. It turns out that the white grandmother of the adopted child has a relative living in essentially the same community as the Native American lawyer who is working to return the child to the tribe, a little place on the reservation called Heaven, Oklahoma. It turns out that this white grandmother has Indian blood in her, and she is eligible to become a member of the tribe. The book ends with the child's adopted white grandmother and her natural Native American grandfather falling in love and agreeing to marry. Thus the story seems to argue that the key to resolving conflicts is to realize that we're all really alike despite our differences, that we're all really from Heaven, and we can make a heaven on earth if we just try.

It's a nice sentiment, but if you're a real flesh-and-blood human you have to know that it's a simplification; moreover, it's not the kind of argument that spurs people to see the world in a different way. In fact, this kind of simplification is one of the cultural myths that is spread in order to suppress change. We're okay, it suggests. We're all decent people and we're doing just fine. The sad truth is that decent people who have serious differences often act indecently. To deny that is to dismiss the problem.

Kingsolver tries to show how difficult it is to be a single mother, how hard it is to be poor, and she wishes to encourage an enlightened view of Native American people and culture. But by failing to invest the novel with adequate seriousness, she has created a book that perpetuates the very problems it purports to address; which is to say, this book, written by a liberal in order to make a liberal argument, ultimately has a reactionary effect.

In the novels Kingsolver has written since, she seems to have consciously worked to achieve the kind of seriousness *Pigs in Heaven* lacks. Moreover, I need to add my own mea culpa, as I have committed a similar literary sin.

In my novel *American Owned Love,* I wanted to explore the very real existence of *colonias* in the Southwest—unincorporated communities that lacked the most basic of services, including running water, electricity, and sewer systems. These colonias typically came about from real estate scams, and some had thousands of residents before state and federal governments took real steps to address the problem (not that the problem has been solved, but it is being addressed).

In my novel, a colonia exists just across the river from the city of Persimmon, New Mexico. The local newspaper is leading a campaign to have it condemned and destroyed, with the residents deported or relocated. An editor approaches one of my principal characters, Gay Schaefer, asking for her support in the campaign. Because her daughter has been assaulted by someone from the colonia, her support would pack an emotional (and racially charged) punch. Gay dismisses the editor in no uncertain terms, and the reader is encouraged to side with her and share some portion of her indignation.

However, shortly thereafter Gay is approached by a woman introduced earlier in the novel. This woman had asked Gay for help, and Gay has ignored her. Without going into all of the details of the plot, it was my intention for Gay's behavior with this woman to embody the same kind of human disregard that she has previously condemned. I meant for the reader's initial identification with Gay's self-righteousness to make the reader feel complicit in the error.

It sounds like it should work, doesn't it? I was careful to show all of the editor's statements about the colonia to be true within the narrative. I tried to balance the argument, and then indicate how the easy indignation was a trap. However, the razing of the colonia was too powerful an element to be balanced by a personal transgression, and most readers never recognized the complications.

If Kingsolver is guilty of excessive optimism—or perhaps of trying to answer a question rather than simply properly raising it—I am guilty of excessive and false subtlety, an unwarranted faith in craft that is ultimately an act of hubris, and so my own novel fails to tell the truth and expose lies.

After I finished tearing down that garage and had chainsawed the many logs and loaded them in a trailer to be hauled away, I got a notice saying that my neighbor the writer was having a book signing at the local bookstore. It turns out she writes cookbooks.

Is it possible to write a subversive cookbook?

That's a topic for another essay.

I believe the best political fiction should be motivated by parallel desires: to create something of artistic merit and to engage the world in a serious and meaningful manner. The best political fiction does not aim to explore merely the immediate and topical issues, but the underlying human traits that churn through the pages of history like a locomotive.

Intelligent questioning is a subversive act, and much of any writer's motivation to write should be to productively undermine conventional beliefs (the readers' and the writer's own). Everyone should find the work subversive, not just the people with whom the writer has political differences.

Writers cannot pretend to be helpless.

PRIVATE EYE POINT OF VIEW

> *. . . down these mean streets a man must go who is not himself mean, who is neither tarnished nor afraid.*
> —RAYMOND CHANDLER

In the classic noir film *Out of the Past,* two characters have the following exchange:

> "This isn't the way to play it."
> "Why not?"
> " 'Cause it isn't the way to win."
> "Is there a way to win?"
> "Well, there's a way to lose more slowly."

I've always had a soft spot for noir films and particularly those that feature a hard-boiled detective. I grew up reading the Hardy Boys, and I was confident that the books were great literature. The term *soft spot* suggests either that your critical faculties are turned off, or that your brain has a mushy aperture. My own brain has many such swampy foyers. For example, I have a wholly felt, deeply ingrained love for baseball. I possess fifteen different versions of Gershwin's "How Long Has This Been Goin' On?" In our twenty-plus years of marriage, my wife has asked me perhaps a million times how some outfit looks on her, and I've never seen her look anything less than beautiful. In short, there are certain things in this world about which I have no ability to judge.

As someone working to be a literary artist, I got the idea early on that perhaps I should avoid narratives that involved any of my soft spots. The lesson was brought home to me during a workshop when I'd turned in the first chapter of a baseball novel set in the middle 1960s. The story was about two friends—a pitcher and a catcher—who had seemed to be headed toward the major leagues but got derailed. The catcher went into a terrible hitting slump, and the pitcher discovered he could not find the strike zone with anyone else behind the plate. Both washed out of the minors and had used up all of their chances by the time the novel opens. However, the catcher has recently discovered that with the right corrective lenses he can hit the ball again, and this leads the pitcher (the protagonist in this epic) to think they still have a chance to pitch in the *show*. All they have to do is figure out a way to disguise themselves as younger, wholly different people. The catcher (the more literary of the two) has read a book called *Black Like Me,* about a white man who dyes his skin to experience prejudice directly. These aging boys then shave their heads, dye their hides, and go to a tryout camp, where they wow the scouts. The novel was meant to be about people who have to give up their identity to achieve their goals and about race and sports in America. Most of all, the novel was meant to be funny. I wanted to ironically exploit the clichés of the sport while also tossing the pitcher and catcher racially explosive curveballs.

My workshop leader pointed out that the novel would be, essentially, a one-joke book. That didn't bother me too much, but I did notice that the only other person in the class who was excited about it was another baseball addict. I came to understand that I'd never be able to determine when the book was working and when I was merely indulging my love of the game.

I dropped the novel (though I still retain dibs on the story) and resolved to avoid all sports books or novels that make use of sports—even if they are unmistakably literary works. For this reason, I've never read Bernard Malamud's *The Natural*, although I love *The Assistant*, *The Fixer*, and *The Magic Barrel*.

A similar line of reasoning kept me from reading mysteries, even though I had noted that virtually every literary writer I knew read them. For that matter, literary critics and scholars also seemed to love them. Then one afternoon I happened upon the poet Bobby Byrd in a bookstore, and we began talking about contemporary novels that effectively engage race and class. He recommended the novels of Walter Mosley, and when we parted I looked for the books and could not find them. I didn't know to look in the mystery section.

Later that year, my family and I were staying with friends in a cabin in the Tetons, and I was recovering from pneumonia. My ability to hike was limited, so I spent the day on the porch, alternately staring at the mountains and reading. When I ran out of books from my backpack, I drove to Jackson Hole and asked a bookseller for books by Walter Mosley. She was a fan and advised me to start with *Devil in a Blue Dress*, the first of the Mosley novels featuring Easy Rawlins. I read it all afternoon and into the night. The next day I was back to buy everything in the store written by Walter Mosley.

As the summer progressed, I tried out other mystery writers but didn't immediately find any to match Mosley. I tossed aside most of them after twenty or thirty pages. For reasons I couldn't then identify, I much preferred the hard-boiled mysteries to the others, and I understood that I needed to read the masters. I found *The Big Sleep* in that same Jackson Hole bookstore, and I wound up reading the entire works of Raymond Chandler before the summer was over. Soft spot or no, I understood that these novels were brilliant works.

Responding to the suggestion that the mystery, by definition, could never become a work of literary art, Raymond Chandler himself offered the following: "Everything written with vitality expresses that vitality; there are no dull subjects, only dull minds." He published the essay containing this defense in the *Atlantic Monthly* in 1945. A little better than six decades later, no defense is required. He and his hard-boiled predecessor Dashiell Hammett are members in good standing of the literary canon. A persuasive argument could be made for Mosley, Ross Macdonald, and James Ellroy to join them, and a few more are knocking at the door: James Lee Burke, Martin Cruz Smith, and a handful of others.

In the same essay quoted above ("The Simple Art of Murder"), Chandler argues that the hard-boiled genre evolved as a response to the unlikely plots and genteel sensibility of what he calls the "classic mystery," meaning the works of such writers as Agatha Christie and Dorothy Sayers. He is slightly kinder to Arthur Conan Doyle, but the hard-boiled detective is unmistakably a reaction against Sherlock Holmes and his ilk, as well. The hard-boiled genre is meant to be more realistic and grittier than these mysteries, with less contrivance in the plot and greater attention paid to the realistic portrayal of crime and detection.

The combination of greater realism and less contrivance shifts the emphasis onto character development, which makes hard-boiled novels more like literary novels. Yet they retain requirements that stem from the genre. The most basic ones would seem to be the following: there has to be a crime, an investigation of the crime, and a resolution of the crime. The criminal must be dealt some portion of justice. Because the mystery has to be solved and justice (at least to some extent) has to be served, it is a structurally conservative genre; that is, the restoration of the status quo is central to all mysteries.

Hard-boiled mysteries rarely have much to do with the tangible kinds of clues that dominate earlier mysteries, most notably Doyle's Sherlock Holmes series. In every story, Holmes inevitably makes a statement that befuddles Dr. Watson, and then explains how he deduced it logically from the clues he has observed. Watson functions as surrogate for the reader, suggesting that we would have missed them, too, and only the great Holmes could put them together. In "A Scandal in Bohemia," Holmes notes that Watson has been getting himself "very wet lately" and that he has "a most clumsy and careless servant girl." Watson is astonished at the accuracy of the deduction and suggests that Holmes would have been burned as a witch in another time. He wants to know how the great detective achieved his insights.

> "It is simplicity itself," said he; "my eyes tell me that on the inside of your left shoe, just where the firelight strikes it, the leather is scored by six almost parallel cuts. Obviously they have been caused by someone who has very carelessly scraped round the edges of the sole in order to remove crusted mud from it. Hence, you see, my double deduction that you had been out in vile weather, and that you had a particularly malignant boot-slitting specimen of the London slavey."

Holmes goes on to tell Watson, "You see, but you do not observe. The distinction is clear."

Hard-boiled detectives don't "observe" any better than Watson. They have no special powers of investigation. If you've ever wondered why, in Dashiell Hammett's *The Maltese Falcon,* Sam Spade refuses to look over the crime site where his partner has been murdered, you now have your answer. Hammett wanted to distinguish his detective from the likes of Holmes immediately. About his dead partner's body, Spade says to the police detective, "You've seen him. You'd see everything I could." This stance is not only more realistic, it permits the hard-boiled dick to be less than a genius.

Instead of looking for clues, hard-boiled detectives read people and speculate on human motives. (Again, this distinction pushes the genre in the direction of literary novels.) It's rare that they study the times people arrived and left or the details of the begonia garden that have subtly changed. Chandler would eventually produce a set of rules for the mystery novel, including the following:

> The mystery novel must be credibly motivated both as to the original situation and the denouement.
> The mystery story must be technically sound about the methods of murder and detection.
> [The mystery novel] must be realistic as to character, setting and atmosphere.
> The mystery novel must have a sound story value apart from the mystery element.
> The mystery novel must punish the criminal in one way or another, not necessarily by operation of the law courts.

Virtually all of Chandler's rules have to do with realism, but contemporary readers will likely balk at calling the Marlowe novels realistic. Certainly they are more realistic than the old-style mysteries, but much of the dialogue is stylized and Marlowe is such a romantic idealist (despite being a tough guy) that one can't help but feel a few steps away from the genuine grit of reality. One could argue that the "police procedural" has evolved in response to the hard-boiled detective genre for the same reasons that the hard-boiled genre came into being. As the term *procedural* suggests, the genre is meant to be even more realistic than Chandler's mean streets. It may be that "true crime" and reality-television crime shows have evolved in response to the popularity of police procedurals for, yet again, identical grounds. However, I'll argue that the mystery novels that have the best chance of achieving something remarkable are those that find middle ground, that are neither dismissible as works of realism nor essentially fictional documentaries.[1]

------

1. I am not here addressing the "nonfiction novel," a genre with undeniably great works, such as Truman Capote's *In Cold Blood*, Joseph Wambaugh's *The Onion Field*, and David Simon's *Homicide*; I'm restricting my examination to fiction.

The hard-boiled detective lives by a code, and that code is essentially chivalric. Much has been made of the connection between the knight in shining armor and the hard-boiled dick in his bad suit. Unlike the knights of old, however, the hard-boiled knight serves neither king nor god. In fact, he serves whoever ambles into his office with enough feed to cover twenty-five-a-day plus expenses. How is that realistic? Why would he risk his life, break the law, get sapped, slapped, and bopped in the kisser, out of loyalty to a client who fairly often turns out to be one of the crooks?

I have a partial answer to this question, which I'm building toward, but for the moment I'll argue that the requirement for hard-boiled detectives to possess a rare kind of integrity and a specific kind of romantic vision has led to a great deal of sentimentality in the genre, mostly of the tough-guy/tender-guy mode. The best writers understand this potential and work to undercut the mush with irony and humor. Sam Spade, for example, must, according to his code, "do something" about the death of his partner, and so his investigation into the Maltese Falcon is energetic and driven. However, Hammett undercuts the likelihood of sentimentality by having Spade acknowledge that his partner was a heel. For that matter, Spade has been having an affair with the guy's wife and has decided that she's a loser as well. Spade is on a romantic mission, but there's nothing pure or earnest about his stance.

I want to add a rule to Chandler's list: The hard-boiled detective novel must be told from a single point of view.[2]

The hard-boiled mystery must be told from the detective's point of view, permitting the reader to be privy to all—or virtually all—the information the detective gathers at the same time that the detective gets it. This puts some remarkable demands on the writer and the narrative. If the reader is getting all the information the detective is getting, it provides the illusion that the reader

------

2. There are plenty of good mysteries with multiple viewpoints, but I don't think they're genuinely hard-boiled.

could solve the mystery, and since the detective is not an analytical genius, it permits the reader to inhabit the same playing field as the detective with what feels like equal status.

At the same time, the writer has to make certain that the reader does not get ahead of the detective. Nothing is worse than reading a mystery and realizing what the detective ought to see or do and then having to wait a hundred pages until the light-bulb finally goes on over his hard-boiled head. Here, then, is one of the essential tensions for the mystery writer: how do you provide the reader with all the necessary information for the solution of the mystery yet keep the detective one step ahead of the reader?

Limited to a single point of view, the hard-boiled detective novel is almost always either in the third-person limited or the first person. Hammett's *The Maltese Falcon* is written in the third-person objective point of view, meaning that Hammett provides no thoughts for any of the characters. It's also called the "fly on the wall" or camera point of view. For obvious reasons, it is often compared to the screenplay. While the objective point of view isn't necessarily focused on one character, *The Maltese Falcon* is limited to Sam Spade. The narrator records nothing that Spade couldn't see or hear, except descriptions of Sam Spade himself. All the descriptions have a hard-boiled slant to them; yet it is a misreading to suggest that the descriptions are filtered through Spade's sensibility. Here's the opening to *The Maltese Falcon:*

> Samuel Spade's jaw was long and bony, his chin a jutting V under the more flexible V of his mouth. His nostrils curved back to make another, smaller, V. His yellow-grey eyes were horizontal. The V *motif* was picked up again by thickish brows rising outward from twin creases above a hooked nose, and his pale brown hair grew down—from high flat temples—in a point on his forehead. He looked rather pleasantly like a blond satan.

This is not Spade's self-estimation, but the opinion of the implied narrator. He is not privy to Spade's thoughts and feelings, but he can let the reader know when Spade is smiling "wolfishly" or "pleasantly, as if nothing serious were involved." The narrator can advise the reader that Miss Wonderly's clothing has been chosen to highlight her eyes, or that the pockets of an overcoat "bulged more than his hands need have made them bulge"; the opinions are limited to what a knowledgeable and opinionated observer might pick up.

The second chapter opens in a manner that emphasizes the cinematic quality of the objective point of view:

A telephone-bell rang in darkness. When it had rung three times bed-springs creaked, fingers fumbled on wood, something small and hard thudded on a carpeted floor, the springs creaked again, and a man's voice said:

"Hello. . . . Yes, speaking. . . . Dead? . . . Yes. . . . Fifteen minutes. Thanks."

A switch clicked and a white bowl hung on three gilded chains from the ceiling's center filled the room with light. Spade, barefooted in green and white checked pajamas, sat on the side of his bed. He scowled at the telephone on the table while his hands took from beside it a packet of brown papers and a sack of Bull Durham tobacco.

This point-of-view decision makes the book weird and exciting. Most writers, when they think of the objective point of view, will name Hemingway's "Hills Like White Elephants." This very short story records a conversation between two travelers, circling around what is not said. The reader must interpret and deduce what the two are really talking about; in this way, it is a kind of mystery itself. The story was published a scant three years before *The Maltese Falcon,* and there can be little question about the similarity in styles between Hemingway and Hammett. While the influence of Hemingway on Hammett seems obvious to me, many argue that it's the other way around, that Hammett's style pre-dates Hemingway's. This argument is less interesting to me than the connection. Hammett and Hemingway narrate their novels in a comparable, hard-edged style.

The objective point of view works wonderfully in *The Maltese Falcon* because the reader's interest in the mystery is strong enough to balance against the absence of any interior life. This point of view may account for the nearly perfect move from book to film, as well. And it provides an elegant means for navigating the tension between showing everything and staying ahead of the reader. You never know what Sam Spade is thinking, so you can't be skeptical when he's made connections that you've missed.

But the objective point of view has not become the dominant mode in hard-boiled novels for a couple of reasons. Here's an obvious one: it is very difficult to manage. Most writers simply couldn't control it for an entire novel without driving a reader crazy. Interiority in the point of view is the specific advantage the fiction writer has over the filmmaker, and it cannot be cast off capriciously.

Moreover, most hard-boiled mysteries are serials, and it becomes much more difficult to keep the objective point of view afloat novel after novel. *The Maltese Falcon* is the only novel featuring Sam Spade. Everything we know about Sam's private life—his affair with his partner's wife, for example—has to be directly embodied in the plot. This makes for great compression, but it limits what you can do if you want to return to the character for another go, and it might encourage such an emphasis on plot that the mysteries would have to become increasingly contrived—exactly the thing the genre is a reaction against.

In "The Simple Art of Murder," Raymond Chandler acknowledges Hammett somewhat grudgingly:

> How original a writer Hammett really was it isn't easy to decide now, even if it mattered. He was one of a group—

the only one who achieved critical recognition—who wrote or tried to write realistic mystery fiction. All literary movements are like this; some one individual is picked out to represent the whole movement; he is usually the culmination of the movement. Hammett was the ace performer, but there is nothing in his work that is not implicit in the early novels and short stories of Hemingway.

As if he's heard the tone of his assessment, Chandler adds, "Yet, for all I know, Hemingway may have learned something from Hammett." Chandler then praises Hammett mightily:

> Hammett gave murder back to the kind of people that commit it for reasons, not just to provide a corpse; and with the means at hand, not hand-wrought dueling pistols, curare and tropical fish. . . . He was spare, frugal, hard-boiled, but he did over and over again what only the best writers can ever do at all. He wrote scenes that seemed never to have been written before.

Hammett's direct influence on Chandler is most evident early on in his career. Chandler's first published story ("Blackmailers Don't Shoot") is written in the third-person objective point of view, and even the rhythms of the sentences recall Hammett's prose. The opening paragraph to the story follows:

> The man in the powder-blue suit—which wasn't powder-blue under the lights of the *Club Bolivar*—was tall, with wide-set gray eyes, a thin nose, a jaw of stone. He had a rather sensitive mouth. His hair was crisp and black, ever so faintly touched with gray, as by an almost diffident hand. His clothes fitted him as though they had a soul of their own, not just a doubtful past. His name happened to be Mallory.

Chandler is quick to make his work distinctive. The Philip Marlowe novels are told from the first-person point of view, and this has become the dominant mode in the genre. There are seven Marlowe novels, an essential difference from the one-shot Spade oeuvre. Chandler's narration is not at all spare or frugal, and it doesn't read anything like Hemingway's work, which he may have admired but which he also liked to ridicule. One of Chandler's early stories is called "The Sun Also Sneezes," and he pokes stylistic fun at Hemingway in the following scene from *Farewell, My Lovely.* Marlowe has been picked up at the house of a quack he's investigating, and he begins calling one of the cops who hauls him off "Hemingway." As they're driving down the hill, the cops talk to him.

> The big man said: "Now that we are all between pals and no ladies present we really don't give so much time to why you went back up there, but this Hemingway stuff is what really has me down."
>
> "A gag," I said. "An old, old gag."
>
> "Who is this Hemingway person at all?"
>
> "A guy that keeps saying the same thing over and over until you begin to believe it must be good."
>
> "That must take a hell of a long time," the big man said. "For a private dick you certainly have a wandering kind of mind. Are you still wearing your own teeth?"

Raymond Chandler's answer to the tension of showing versus knowing sounds simple: he has his first-person point-of-view character provide all the details that are necessary for the reader to know about the mystery, and he keeps the reader from getting ahead of the detective by providing far more details than are absolutely necessary. This is a realistic strategy. A real crime site may well hold many valuable clues but it will also be chock-full of nonessential information.

But this solution creates problems. It demands that the author ignore certain rules of economy, rules that are embodied in the spare writing of Ernest Hemingway. Chandler writes lengthy and elaborate descriptions of people and places that may, ultimately, have little or nothing to do with the outcome of the mystery. How does he manage to get away with it? Take a look at the following passage from *The Big Sleep:*

A single drop light burned far back, beyond an open, once gilt elevator. There was a tarnished and well-missed spittoon on a gnawed rubber mat. A case of false teeth hung on the mustard-colored wall like a fuse box in a screen porch. I shook the rain off my hat and looked at the building directory beside the case of teeth. Numbers with names and numbers without names. Plenty of vacancies or plenty of tenants who wished to remain anonymous. Painless dentists, shyster detective agencies, small sick businesses that had crawled there to die, mail order schools that would teach you how to become a railroad clerk or a radio technician or a screen writer—if the postal inspectors didn't catch up with them first. A nasty building in which the smell of stale cigar butts would be the cleanest odor.

An old man dozed in the elevator, on a ramshackle stool, with a burst-out cushion under him. His mouth was open, his veined temples glistened in the weak light. He wore a blue uniform coat that fitted him the way a stall fits a horse. Under that gray trousers with frayed cuffs, white cotton socks and black kid shoes, one of which was slit across a bunion. On the stool he slept miserably, waiting for a customer. I went past him softly, the clandestine air of the building prompting me, found the fire door and pulled it open. The fire stairs hadn't been swept in a month. Bums had slept on them, eaten on them, left crusts and fragments of greasy newspaper, matches, a gutted imitation-leather pocketbook. In a shadowy angle against the scribbled wall a pouched ring of pale rubber had fallen and had not been disturbed. A very nice building.

These are wonderfully entertaining paragraphs and the details create a strong sense of place, but none of these details will turn out to be of any particular importance to the mystery. The reader needs to know that Marlowe gets upstairs unobserved, but that hardly accounts for the case of false teeth, the elevator operator whose "veined temples glistened in the weak light," the gutted pocketbook, or the discarded condom. Sherlock Holmes would lose his mind in the Fulwider Building, as there are enough clues to choke a horse.

The reader doesn't know what's important, so she likely thinks she's reading information that's pertinent to the plot. That tension helps, of course, but it isn't enough to drag a reader through long passages of sheer description. Chandler's solution is to make the descriptions valuable in and of themselves. He makes the descriptions entertaining by using humor and lyricism to create an atmosphere and reveal the character of Marlowe. That the detective would take special notice of the world around him is consistent with his calling—he's paid to pay attention. And if he's going to provide that many details, we come to think that the things being described have some kind of larger importance. The setting and the atmosphere are so thoroughly described and evoked that they become more important in hard-boiled novels than in most mysteries—than in most any kind of novel.

Clearly, Chandler's model is not Hemingway and not really Hammett and obviously not Agatha Christie or Arthur Conan Doyle. His favorite novel was *The Great Gatsby,* and it seems very likely that he used it as a model for his first two novels, *The Big Sleep* and *Farewell, My Lovely.*

The plot of *The Great Gatsby* sounds a lot like a mystery. There are two murders in it, and the title character is a gangster attempting to appear respectable for his own reasons. The novel is in the first-person point of view, and the voice is lyrical and often very funny. In the first chapter, the narrator calls on a house of great wealth in which he encounters two beautiful women and a powerful man. There is a mysterious phone call, a rumor about an affair, and the narrator recalls dimly that there was some sort of bad publicity a while back about one of the women. In fact, one of these women will be revealed as a murderer by novel's end. Eventually, Nick Carraway will become an agent for Gatsby in his quest to win back Daisy, arranging a meeting between them.

The Big Sleep opens with Marlowe arriving at the Sternwood mansion. He will encounter two beautiful women and a powerful man. One of these women will be revealed to be the murderer. The man who has been killed (the reader eventually discovers) is the husband of one of the women, a roughneck of a different social class. The elements of Fitzgerald's book have been tossed about, but many of the essential outlines are still evident.

Farewell, My Lovely shows the influence even more completely. Like Gatsby, Moose Malloy is a gangster who has been separated from the love of his life by unavoidable circumstances. Military service took Gatsby away. For Moose, it was doing a stretch in the big house. During this absence, the woman Moose loves has married a man of great wealth and power. Like Nick, Marlowe becomes a reluctant agent for the gangster. The women in question will each betray her old flame, commit a murder, and be responsible (directly or indirectly) for the death of her former lover—while the gangster heroes remain true to their women unto death. In both cases, this loyalty redeems them in the eyes of the narrator.

Social class is a major theme in *The Great Gatsby*, and it has become the most pervasive thematic element in hard-boiled novels since Chandler. It is a crucial element, as a detective who goes down only the mean streets and never finds darkness elsewhere would inadvertently make an ugly class statement. In Chandler's work, Marlowe haunts both sides of the tracks, and the sleaze he finds in the run-down shanties is more than equaled by the corruption and moral squalor he uncovers among the wealthy.[3]

In the opening pages of *The Great Gatsby,* Nick recalls advice from his father about withholding judgment. Marlowe does not have this luxury. This is the crucial difference between the narrators, and it is so extreme that it does not seem accidental. Because the hard-boiled detective is not much interested in tangible clues, he must rely on the intangible ones—those having to do with his understanding of human nature. His ability to measure others is his greatest asset. But since the writer must not give away who the real suspects are by lavishing attention only on them, this same judgmental quality infuses the descriptions of all the characters, all the locales, all the interiors—everything. Ultimately, what emerges from this process is the requirement that every line of the novel be imbued with this very judgmental character's vision of the world. It is in everything he sees and reports, and it's in every word he speaks. And it is this, I would argue, that makes the work of Raymond Chandler transcend the genre, as this requirement is identical to that of literary fiction written in the first person.

Here's how Carmen Sternwood is described in the opening pages of *The Big Sleep:*

> She was twenty or so, small and delicately put together, but she looked durable. She wore pale blue slacks and they looked well on her. She walked as if she were floating. Her hair was a fine tawny wave cut much shorter than the current fashion of pageboy tresses curled in at the bottom.

------

3. Chandler's emulators have continued this scrutiny of class, and Walter Mosley has written some of the most celebrated and effective political novels of the past few decades. The crucial element for success that many of Mosley's imitators fail to understand is that Mosley remains scrupulously true to the demands of the genre, including that of economy. This is the prime reason that the political commentary is so effective; the politics are crucial to the mystery, and so the political content never seems imposed, superfluous, or moralizing.

Her eyes were slate-gray, and had almost no expression when they looked at me. She came over near me and smiled with her mouth and she had little sharp predatory teeth, as white as fresh orange pith and as shiny as porcelain. They glistened between her thin too taut lips. Her face lacked color and didn't look too healthy.

"Tall, aren't you?" she said.

"I didn't mean to be."

Her eyes rounded. She was puzzled. She was thinking. I could see, even on that short acquaintance, that thinking was always going to be a bother to her.

The genre demands for Marlowe to be extremely judgmental, and it is this extremity that makes the narrative powerful.

Some of Chandler's tricks give themselves up to scrutiny. For example, he will take a common description—a cliché, even—an extra step, pushing to make it both more decisive and funny. A very familiar line, such as, "The carpet was so thick I had to wade through it," becomes, "You could just manage to walk on the carpet without waders." An ordinary description of nausea, such as, "I was feeling better, though my stomach was still swinging and swaying a little, but not as bad as before," becomes, "I was in good shape again. I was almost sober and my stomach was bunting toward third base instead of trying for the centerfield flagpole." An utterly typical description of a dump, such as, "Inside was a long dark hallway that hadn't been mopped in a long time," becomes, "Inside was a long dark hallway that had been mopped the day McKinley was inaugurated."

There may be times that we don't care for Marlowe's vision or times that it seems corny, but ultimately, these things do nothing to undercut the experience of spending hours at a time inhabiting this very specific and fully imagined vision. Typically, when we write from the first person, our characters are not nearly so judgmental, or if they are, we're careful to show that they're misreading the world most of the time, or that they're crazy, or that they're unbearable. But first-person judgmental is often a sign of a great novel. Think, for example, of *Lolita* and that extreme and utterly engrossing vision of the world; you don't have to buy into it to be affected by it.

In my experience, the creative process tends to work something like the following: *1 leads to 2, which, in turn, changes 1.* A combination of demands requires that Marlowe must be a person who describes things at length and through a very specific and decisive viewpoint; this, then, serves to define who he is, and the sheer amount of space taken up by the description of place suggests something like a love for it. Marlowe's knightly business permits him to inhabit his realm in a meaningful way—even though most of what is meaningful stems from his manner of inhabiting it. This is my explanation for why Marlowe stays true to his code; it doesn't matter who hires him because the real mystery is about having a meaningful way to engage the world, and—to borrow from *Gatsby*—it is a world filled with "enchanted objects."

In this sense, Marlowe is Nick *and* Gatsby, but his romantic vision has no single Daisy at the center of it; rather, it is his idealized vision of worthy damsels and men of honor that fuels his "colossal vitality," along with a dark and haunting landscape imbued with magic by his apprehension of it.

What any literary writer can take away from studying the best hard-boiled mysteries has to do with the formal demands of a genre, and how they may actually free a writer even while seeming to encumber him. Poets have long argued about forms and free verse, but for writers who work exclusively in free verse, the idea of formal demands can be powerfully appealing.

Beyond this specific scrutiny, the study of these mysteries rewards the serious reader in the same manner as any other work of literature—by providing a world with its own style and rules and magic.

* * *

"You know, the law isn't for people like us."

"What is?"

"Well, that's another thing I've been trying to figure out for years."

(Dialogue from noir film *Marked Woman,* starring Bette Davis and Humphrey Bogart.)

This essay refers to the following creative works:
One Hundred Years of Solitude by Gabriel García Márquez
"The Housebreaker of Shady Hill" by John Cheever

- 175 -

YOU MUST CHANGE YOUR LIFE

Once upon a time I had a hideout. It was my home.

Our house was a bad house surrounded by a splendid waste-land. We lived in Arizona, between Tucson and Ajo, in the middle of the vast Sonora Desert: one hundred thousand square miles of cover. A lush place, by wasteland standards, with palo verde and mesquite, saguaro and creosote, yucca, organ pipe, prickly pear, ocotillo, sage. A few other bad houses and a scatter of squat trail-ers pustuled the desert nearby, but we were largely alone in our little dump, except for the coyotes and sidewinders, scorpions and tarantulas, the rare Gila monster. Our conclave of ugliness was not easy to find, and few humans had reason to attempt it. To get to our house required a dozen unlikely turns on streets unpaved and unmarked, prone to drifting sand and flashing flood, hazards to the uninitiated, the unknowing, the unintrepid, and (most sig-nificant for this tale) the police.

We were twenty-three and twenty-two, not quite penniless, not entirely brainless, on the downward arc of a trainer marriage. Our house was made of what we westerners call "slump block," the cheapest material in the history of shelter. Slump block is the building equivalent of Old Milwaukee beer or Mad Dog 20-20 wine—both of which I sold at the convenience store where I was employed, the U-Tote-M on Miracle Mile, just down from the bowling alley, right across from the escort service, not far from the No-Tel Motel. Minimum wage, high risk. Your one-stop Slim Jim, Pampers, and booze emporium.

My wife waitressed, starting at the bottom (i.e., Bob's Big Boy) and working her way up to a Mediterranean restaurant with belly dancers and cloth napkins. We both worked nights. I volunteered for the swing and graveyard shifts. My friend Clam (not his real name), who had got me on at the U-Tote-M, advised in favor of these hours. "More time to study," he explained. Clam was an undergraduate at the University of Arizona.

My wife and I were undergraduates at virtually everything. Our grades in most subjects were less than stellar. We hadn't known, when we enrolled, what all would be required. In House-keeping 101, we earned a collective D. Poor participation hurt us. In Interior Design, we made a stronger effort. My wife sewed curtains our first week in the house, and she hung them up to measure their length before hemming them. They remained hanging, un-hemmed and unraveling, for the three years of our habitation. For my part, I snatched a faux marble countertop from the Dumpster when the U-Tote-M remodeled. We centered it on cinder blocks and put decorative ashtrays over the gashes and cigarette scars. Our couch we discovered curbside on garbage day, the springs marshmallowed on either end but were firm in the middle, a frowning mustard-colored steal. Overall grade: D+.

We did a little better at some of the more esoteric subjects:

Keeping the Electricity from Being Shut Off: C
Putting Gas in the Car So We Didn't Run Out in the
     Middle of the Desert: C−
Changing the Cooler Pads: Incomplete

At the actual university, we showed only slightly more competence. We took turns going full-time and working part-time, and then vice versa. I was enrolled in the little-known five-and-a-half year baccalaureate plan. It was an arduous program of all-night cramming followed by sleeping through exams, of inspired essays handed in on the wrong dates, of dreaming during Psych 301 that my professor was at the U-Tote-M cash register asking for Piaget cigarettes, only to wake and find my classmates halfway through a test on Skinner's pigeons and Pavlov's slobbering dogs. I was likely drooling myself, but it got me no extra credit.

I was a psychology major because I had the desperate hope that if I took enough psych courses I could discover what was wrong with me and why I couldn't get my act together.

It wasn't working.

I knew that I wanted to be a writer, and I took workshops. But something about my writing was inadequate, something more than my inability to spell and semioccasional fling with grammar, something more than my wobbly characters and nineteenth-century diction. (I loved Melville.)

My greatest literary success of the time: I could drink in a fashion that emulated Faulkner.

Our pudgy slump-block house had a pebbled roof covering three bedrooms. When my wife's sister needed a place to live, naturally she moved in with us. Shortly afterward, Clam showed up at the door bearing a plastic garbage bag filled with all his possessions. He had run into some trouble in a business transaction of questionable legality (he was selling pot and the deal went sour), and he needed to disappear for a while. He required a hideout and we had one.

Clam claimed the remaining bedroom, and for a long time he neither left the house nor stepped in front of an open window. It was hard to measure the actual threat he was under from unhappy associates or vice detectives. It was his habit to exaggerate his emotional responses in the most conventional manner possible. He threw his arms up in alarm. His knees wobbled with anxiety. He slapped his thigh when he laughed. He ducked under windows when hiding from the law. My wife and I had different ideas about this trait. I thought it embodied his idea of humor—the expected inflated comically by its own predictability. My wife believed it was how he compensated for shallow feelings, simultaneously his apology and his excuse for being a man.

We both liked him. He gave us a topic.

Clam did what he could to entertain himself—smoking joints and playing records while watching muted television approximately twenty-two hours of the day. He had powerful feelings about music, television, and certain games—chess, spades, Scrabble, pinochle. For that matter, he felt passionately about almost anything that did not require rising from the sofa. Clam was fervently lethargic.

From his sofa perch, he fell in love with my sister-in-law. There were good reasons for him to fall. She was friendly, smart, and beautiful. Also, he was afraid to leave the house, and she was the only unmarried woman who lived there.

It seemed to him that fate had thrown them together.

She quite decidedly declined to see it that way.

Clam worked hard, relatively speaking, to win her heart. He played albums he thought she would like. He bellowed for her when certain TV shows came on. While the rest of us were out working or going to classes, he scribbled in a notebook—pickup lines specifically contoured to her liking—comparing her eyes to the eyes of her favorite sitcom star, making suggestive comments in the style of a talk-show host she admired.

Over the course of their first few months together, Clam made precisely zero progress. He thought the hitch was merely that she didn't like him. I suggested the problem had a quality of the *macro* about it.

The next thing that happened also seemed to him an act of fate. I gave him a book to read: *One Hundred Years of Solitude* by Gabriel García Márquez.

Over the next few days, the household underwent a metamorphosis. The air became breathable. Only instrumentals played on the stereo. The TV gave up its silent dominion. Even when Clam momentarily put the novel down, he would talk about nothing else. He tried to engage my sister-in-law in a discussion of literature, but she wouldn't go for it. This did not discourage his pursuit of her. Nothing discouraged it.

A couple of weeks into this new stage of our lives, I happened to see the book propped open on the coffee table. He was less than halfway through it. I kidded him about making such a production of a novel he had only just begun.

He corrected me. He was reading it a second time.

A few days later, he asked me to take him into town. I expressed surprise that he was willing to risk a drive. It was the first time he had considered leaving the hideout. He told me he needed to find a bookstore that carried Spanish titles. He wanted to read the novel in its original language.

Let me pause here to say that I cradled a tender and controversial belief that Clam was an intelligent person. He simply had no expression for his intelligence. None whatsoever. The traditional routes proved too inflexible for his intellectual acumen. Standardized tests were coarse measurements, after all, and the university routinely deterred scholarly aspirations by means of its rigid adherence to outdated requirements, such as homework and class attendance. Professors would not even consider his theories on REM-mode learning in the classroom. All of which is to say: I couldn't believe that Clam was dumb without thinking the same about myself.

Yet I couldn't entirely ignore that Clam had flunked introductory Spanish twice. For that matter, he had flunked English (his native language) three times. Hence, when he asked me to take him to a Spanish bookstore, I felt obliged to call attention to the following: "You don't know Spanish."

He shrugged. "I'm gonna get a dictionary, too."

Over the next several weeks, Clam labored through *Cien años de soledad*. It was no small undertaking. He transcribed sentences in pencil, paging through the dictionary for each word to create a literal translation. He then calculated what the sentence must actually mean in the context of the story. He could only rarely consult the English-language version because he had lent it to my sister-in-law, convinced that García Márquez would be the weld that would join them.

I was there the momentous afternoon when Clam asked my sister-in-law how far she was into the novel. The room was bright. Clam and I were slouched on the surly yellow couch, reading books and listening to Doc and Merle Watson on the stereo. The drawn curtains caused the desert light to decant along the window's edges, splashing the bare walls, providing the room with a gilt propriety it did not deserve. I had recently switched my major from psychology to English. I'd had classes back-to-back, studying Freud for one hour, and then Melville the next. The juxtaposition made it clear to me that Melville knew more about the human heart than Freud could dream of knowing. I switched to English, thinking that if I took enough literature courses I might discover what was wrong with me and why I couldn't get my act together.

My sister-in-law entered the room in her nightgown, a diaphanous, insect-colored concoction of ruffles that almost reached her thighs. She wore it often. Clam had privately described the gown as the physical embodiment of *haze* because it obscured but did not hide the landscape. He had the theory that she "clothed" herself in this outfit specifically to give him hope. That it was *hot* and none of us wore much did not in any way deter his faith. He took the nightgown as a good sign. That she had slept late meant she had stayed up all night devouring the book. I understood his logic. The success of his plan seemed ready to light upon his lap. He braved a pair of questions.

"How's the reading going?" he asked. "What part are you at?"

"I quit reading it," she told him.

His mouth dropped open. The book tumbled from his hands. His eyes grew as wide and round as handcuffs. He did the obligatory sidelong at me, speechless.

I had to be the one to ask why she'd quit.

She had reached the point in the novel where one of the characters ties himself to a tree and takes to eating dirt.

"That's a *great* part," Clam said.

"People don't eat dirt," she replied. "It's not realistic."

Clam had no ready gesture to respond to this. He had to actually think. It took several seconds. "Haven't you ever felt so low," he asked, "so bad about yourself or something you've done, that you could just eat dirt?"

"No," she said. She did not hesitate or elaborate. Instead, she crossed her arms. No one was going to tell her that she had ever felt like eating dirt or that she ever would.

I believed her. With great reluctance, Clam came to believe her, too. She put down the book and, to my knowledge, never picked it up again. Clam's infatuation with my sister-in-law was over.

His love affair with the novel, however, had only just begun. He enrolled in a Spanish class to get help with the translation. That summer he went to Guadalajara to study for six weeks. Within a few months, he had moved to Guadalajara. He lived there for two years, and then returned to the University of Arizona to complete a degree in Spanish, a scant decade after his initial matriculation.

One Hundred Years of Solitude had been recommended to me by one of my creative-writing teachers. I was taking as many fiction and poetry workshops as I could fit into my schedule, and unlike in my other studies, I always managed to be awake and prepared for class. If someone had told me that for the bulk of my adult life I would earn my living by teaching such workshops, I would have laughed. I would have thought it impossible. In my first workshop, I earned the grade of C. (*Earned* is the key word in the previous sentence.) It was undoubtedly the lowest grade in the class. Given that I never missed a workshop and completed all of the assignments, getting a C was much like sending your drawings to one of the matchbook schools and getting a letter saying, "Thanks, but maybe you should look for another kind of outlet." It just didn't happen.

My teacher was the novelist Robert C. S. Downs, a good writer and good teacher, and if I had been a halfway sane student, I could have learned a great deal from him. However, I was not even a quarter-way rational. My desire to become a writer was so huge, and my love of great novels was so true, I thought the salvation of my soul depended on every word I wrote. I turned in a piece of fiction that opened in Africa with a boy being taken into slavery, and then the narrative followed his travel to the United States, his work on a plantation in the South, an incident that inspired him to run away, and his pursuant death from wildlife. If I remember correctly, the story's length was eight pages. Double-spaced.

I found the C in fiction writing discouraging and waited a year before trying another workshop. In the interim I wrote a story about a man living in a rooming house who comes to understand (by means of sexual intercourse with a lovely boarder and the sound of a lonesome train passing in the distance) that life is a sham. In this class, my teacher, Robert Houston, read aloud the first paragraph of my story using a Dracula accent, sticking his tongue out for emphasis. Then he said, "Who can define the term *purple prose*?"

How he knew I could sustain this humiliation, I don't know, but it was exactly the kick in the pants I needed. "Melville and Hawthorne are great writers," he said to me, "but if they were alive today, they would be using the idioms of contemporary language." (Did I mention that I used "thy" and "thou" in the story? Did I let on that the convolutions of my sentences made Henry James look like Hemingway?)

Daunted but undeterred, I began my next story. Like Clam in his pursuit of my sister-in-law, I was in love and an idiot. But I did take the hint. I wrote a story in simple, straightforward language about some high school boys (Clam, me, and a couple of others had a few years earlier lived much of this story) going down to Mexico to the Zona Rosa to see strippers. One of the strippers took an interest in our table, and when she came over, she pressed a friend's head against her crotch. Minutes later, she ripped off her top to reveal that she was a man. That didn't seem enough, so I had the boys hit a strolling drunk on the drive back to the border crossing. The boys paused, but then kept on going, thereby turning small sins into large ones.

It wasn't a good story, but it was about three miles ahead of the rooming-house fiasco. Bob Houston's foot in my behind turned out to be exactly what I'd needed. I have never quite had the nerve to be so bold when I teach, but it was the single most important moment in any classroom in all my life.

Years later, after I finished graduate school, Bob Houston would go out of his way to help me go to the Bread Loaf Writers' Conference with a working scholarship. (I was the most incompetent waiter in Bread Loaf history, but that's another story entirely.) After my first book was published, I was invited to interview for a job at Penn State, where Robert Downs was a professor of creative writing. He called me at home to say that I was his first choice. I asked if he remembered teaching me.

"Of course I do," he said. "You got a C. You were quite the numbskull."

I make a point of telling my undergraduate students about my first workshop. I try to tell them, honestly and exactly, what is wrong with their stories and to make suggestions about what to do next, hoping they can experience the same kind of revelation I did—only without the Dracula overtones. Sometimes I tell them about my friend Clam and me, living in that lousy house with two beautiful sisters, constantly undone by our own hopeless, moronic selves.

Clam, with the help of García Márquez, pulled out of it before I did. While he was in Mexico studying Spanish and reinventing himself, my marriage ended. I had enrolled in graduate school in counseling, making an attempt to impersonate an adult and thereby save our union. However, I didn't fool anybody. I studied to become a counselor, thinking I might discover what was wrong with me and why I couldn't get my act together.

When I finished the program, I accepted a good counseling position in San Diego, where I bought a sports car and lived in an apartment right on the Pacific Ocean. I had a lot of friends (move to the beach and everyone you've ever known is suddenly your pal). I also had a girlfriend who had the whole package—beauty, intelligence, kindness, employment. My job provided me with more money than I could spend. I was living out a certain kind of adolescent fantasy, but I was not happy. My life looked great from the right distance, and yet as its protagonist I was miserable. I still wanted to be a writer, but it didn't seem possible. In fact, it seemed less likely than ever. How could I give up such a desirable life?

On a brilliant summer afternoon I was reclining in a lounge chair on the beach enjoying the sun on my skin, the lulling rhythm of the waves, and the spectacle of parading bodies. I was also reading the collected stories of John Cheever. It's a fat book, and I'd reached page 300, a story called "The Housebreaker of Shady Hill." It is the story of Johnny Hake, a man who loses his way and becomes a thief, but manages to rectify his mistakes before it is too late.

> I wish I could say that a kindly lion had set me straight, or an innocent child, or the strains of distant music from some church, but it was no more than the rain on my head—the smell of it flying up to my nose—that showed me the extent of my freedom from the bones in Fontainebleau and the works of a thief. There were ways out of my trouble if I cared to make use of them. I was not trapped. I was here on earth because I chose to be.

Lying on the beach, reading this story, I began to cry. It's actually a funny story, but it made me cry. I put the book away and took a walk. I heated up a can of soup and ate it directly from the pan. I had a long argument with my pillow about the shape it wished to take about my head. "There were ways out of my trouble if I cared to make use of them. I was not trapped. I was here on earth because I chose to be." Those words kept turning over and over in my mind. By the end of a sleepless night I had decided what I wanted to do with my life: I would give myself a chance to become a writer.

I called for application materials from graduate schools the following Monday. I applied to a dozen of them. When a couple accepted me, I sold my sports car to get rid of the payments. By the time it was summer again, I had told the people I worked with that I was quitting to go back to school. They all wanted to know if they could have my apartment.

If it's fair to call Cheever a literary lion, then for me, it *was* a kindly lion that set me straight. The story of Johnny Hake changed my life. *One Hundred Years of Solitude* changed my friend Clam's life. It's not what literature can do; it's what it must do.

My friend Clam now teaches Spanish in high school. The last time I saw him, he was dating a Brazilian microbiologist who had introduced him to the novels of José Saramago of Portugal.

"They're amazing," Clam told me, throwing his arms open in wonder. "You've got to read them."

He's teaching himself Portuguese.

WORKS REFERENCED

Albee, Edward. *Who's Afraid of Virginia Woolf?*

Boswell, Robert. *American Owned Love*

—. *Living to Be 100*

Bowen, Merlin. "Captain Vere and the Weakness of Expediency." In *Critical Essays on Melville's Billy Budd, Sailor.* Ed. Robert Milder.

Brown, Rosellen. *Before and After*

Brunvand, Jan Harold. *The Baby Train and Other Lusty Urban Legends*

—. *The Choking Doberman*

—. *The Vanishing Hitchhiker*

Chandler, Raymond. *The Big Sleep*

—. *Red Wind*

—. *Raymond Chandler Speaking*

—. *Farewell, My Lovely*

—. *The Simple Art of Murder*

Cheever, John. *The Stories of John Cheever*

Chekhov, Anton Pavlovich. *Letters of Anton Chekhov.* Trans. Constance Garnett.

—. *Notebook of Anton Chekhov.* Trans. S. S. Koteliansky and Leonard Woolf.

Chomsky, Noam. *The Chomsky Reader*

Dark, Alice Elliott. *In the Gloaming*

DeLillo, Don. *White Noise*

Dobyns, Stephen. *Cold Dog Soup*

Doyle, Sir Arthur Conan. *The Complete Sherlock Holmes.* Vol. 1

Fitzgerald, F. Scott. *The Great Gatsby*

Fuhrman tapes, http://web.mit.edu/dryfoo/www/Info/fuhrman
   .html

García Márquez, Gabriel. *One Hundred Years of Solitude.* Trans.
   Gregory Rabassa.

Gazzaniga, Michael. *Nature's Mind: The Biological Roots of
   Thinking, Emotions, Sexuality, Language, and Intelligence*

Gould, Stephen J., and Lewontin, R.C. "The Spandrels of San
   Marco and the Panglossian Paradigm: A Critique of the
   Adaptationist Programme." *Proceedings of the Royal Society
   of London* B 205 (1979): 581–98.

Hammett, Dashiell. *The Maltese Falcon*

Hemingway, Ernest. *The Short Stories of Ernest Hemingway*

Irving, John. *The World According to Garp*

James, Henry. *The Art of Fiction*

Jason, Philip, and Lefcowitz, Allan. *Creative Writer's Handbook*

Johnson, Denis. *Jesus' Son*

Kingsolver, Barbara. *Pigs in Heaven*

Lahiri, Jhumpa. *Interpreter of Maladies*

Le Guin, Ursula K. *The Left Hand of Darkness*

Melville, Herman. *Billy Budd, Sailor*

Miller, Sue. *For Love*

Mosley, Walter. *Devil in a Blue Dress*

Mumford, Lewis. "The Flowering Aloe." *Herman Melville*

Munro, Alice. *Selected Stories*

Nelson, Antonya. *Family Terrorist*

O'Brien, Tim. *The Things They Carried*

O'Connor, Flannery. *A Good Man Is Hard to Find and Other
   Stories*

—. *Mystery and Manners.* Ed. Sally and Robert Fitzgerald

O'Hara, John. *BUtterfield 8*

Purdy, James. *The Nephew*

Robinson, Marilynne. *Housekeeping*

Roth, Philip. *Goodbye, Columbus*

Taylor, Peter. *The Collected Stories of Peter Taylor*

Thompson, Jean. *Who Do You Love*

Tolstoy, Leo. *Anna Karenina.* Trans. Rosemary Edmonds.

—. *Anna Karenina.* Trans. Richard Pevear and Larissa
    Volokhonsky.

—. *The Death of Ivan Ilych.* Trans. Louise and Aylmer Maude.

Wallace, David Foster. *Oblivion*

Weiner, Jonathan. *The Beak of the Finch: A Story of Evolution in
    Our Time*

ROBERT BOSWELL is the author of six novels (including *Century's Son, Mystery Ride,* and *Crooked Hearts*), two story collections, a play, a cyberpunk novel, and a nonfiction book about a treasure hunt—*What Men Call Treasure: The Search for Gold at Victorio Peak.* He has received National Endowment for the Arts fellowships, a Guggenheim Fellowship, the Iowa School of Letters Award for Fiction, the PEN West Award for Fiction, the John Gassner Prize for Playwriting, and the Evil Companions Award. His stories have appeared in the *New Yorker, Best American Short Stories, O. Henry Prize Stories, Pushcart Prize Stories, Epoch, Esquire, Colorado Review,* and many other magazines. Graywolf will publish Boswell's new story collection in May 2009. He is married to the writer, Antonya Nelson, and they have two children, Jade and Noah. Boswell teaches creative writing at New Mexico State University, the University of Houston, and in the Warren Wilson MFA Program.

The Half-Known World has been typeset in Warnock Pro; designed by Robert Slimbach, Warnock Pro is a new Adobe Originals type composition family named after John Warnock, the co-founder of Adobe Systems. This book was designed by Ann Sudmeier. Composition by BookMobile Design and Publishing Services, Minneapolis, Minnesota, and manufactured by Versa Press on acid-free paper.